BEING CHURCH

BEING CHURCH

AN ECCLESIOLOGY FOR THE REST OF US

Pablo R. Andiñach

translated by Ana María Buela

CASCADE *Books* • Eugene, Oregon

BEING CHURCH
An Ecclesiology for the Rest of Us

Copyright © 2014 Pablo R. Andiñach. All rights reserved. Except for brief quotations in critical publications or reviews, no part of this book may be reproduced in any manner without prior written permission from the publisher. Write: Permissions, Wipf and Stock Publishers, 199 W. 8th Ave., Suite 3, Eugene, OR 97401.

Cascade Books
An Imprint of Wipf and Stock Publishers
199 W. 8th Ave., Suite 3
Eugene, OR 97401

www.wipfandstock.com

ISBN 13: 978-1-62032-135-5

Cataloging-in-Publication data:

Andiñach, Pablo R.

    Being church : an ecclesiology for the rest of us / Pablo R. Andiñach ; translated by Ana María Buela.

    xii + 106 p. ; 23 cm. —Includes bibliographical references.

    ISBN 13: 978-1-62032-135-5

    1. Church. 2. Mission of the church. I. Buela, Ana María. II. Title.

BV600.3 .A50 2014

Manufactured in the U.S.A.

Contents

Acknowledgments vii
Introduction ix

PART 1: BEING CHURCH
1. People of God or Body of Christ? 3
2. Being an Evangelical (and Catholic) Church 9
3. Is the Church a Perfect Institution? (Am I Perfect?) 17
4. The Bible: Is It the Word of God? 24
5. A Church without Spirituality? 31
6. The Spirituality of the Believer 38
7. The Missionary Church 45

PART 2: CHRIST AND US
8. Who Do We Say He Is? 55
9. Remembering Our Baptism (Who Am I?) 62
10. The Lord's Table (Who Are We?) 70
11. Proclaiming the Word: The Third Sacrament? 77
12. From What Does Christ Save Us? 84
13. For What Does Christ Saves Us? 91
14. Our Faith and Our Mission: The Pond Begins to Tremble 98

Bibliography 105

Acknowledgments

It was when considering the emptiness that seems to overwhelm current times that the first intuitions to deliver these pages emerged. They intend to rethink old words and gestures that are full of meaning but are also demanding a new approach, a breath of fresh air to revitalize them and put them into action again. They emerge, too, from the belief that it is only when falling that we feel the giddiness of rising, just as thirst provides the opportunity to appreciate how water restores our body. They are, consequently, words that need to be said soon and that seek another in order to grow and develop.

The original manuscript was read and corrected by my colleagues in pastoral ministry and teaching: Arne Clausen, Nancy Bedford (Garret-Evangelical Theological Seminary, Chicago), and Guillermo Hansen (Luther Seminary, Minnesota), also colleagues when teaching at Instituto Universitario ISEDET in Buenos Aires. Also, I want to express my gratitude to the Faith and Order Commission of the World Council of Churches where many of the issues here presented were discussed in its meetings, papers, and consultations. My thanks to my friend and colleague Hugo Magallanes, Director of The Center for the Study of Latino/a Christianity and Religions of Perkins School of Theology, and to The Henry Luce Foundation for their generous contribution in making this translation possible. I want to thank Ana María Buela for her work as translator and Wendi Neal for her careful reading and corrections of the English text. In particular, I want to express my gratitude to William Abraham for his support and help in the process of translation. Further, I am grateful to William Lawrence, Dean of Perkins School of Theology, for the invitation as Visiting Professor

ACKNOWLEDGMENTS

during 2011–2012. This translation is one of the many fruits of the time spent there.

Little, if any, of what one writes can be attributed solely to oneself. I owe this book and its main ideas to those around me, with whom I share the winding ways of the gospel. My past and present teachers are an intangible yet real presence in the ways I approach daily life. From that multitude I would like to especially mention my parents, Esteban and Nilda (she who is already with the Lord), whose love for the gospel and the church is reflected in these pages. It is to them, in representation of many others, that I dedicate this book.

Pablo R. Andiñach
Buenos Aires, August 2014

Introduction

This little book resulted from the conviction that we need to think through what it is to be the church in the contemporary world. We are aware that we are living in a time of crisis, with rapid social and cultural changes that challenge the way we have been a church, challenges that come not only from outside the institution—from the society in which it acts—but from the inside as well. The church is challenged by a secularized society, which tends not to accept institutional authority, but also by those Christians who are looking for alternatives within the church expressed through renewal movements, harsh criticisms coming from the core of the church, and regular calls to change the point of view (oddly enough, some people try to change the so-called traditional point of view, and others want to change "cutting-edge" solutions proposed in the last decades). Society has developed new questions and, to some extent, has modified the cultural context in which the church moves and should proclaim the gospel. Consequently, it is urgent to find the place and mission of the church in this new context. It is necessary to ask and attempt to answer these essential questions: What is the foundation of the church? Who are we? Who is the Christ we believe in? What is the mission of the church? What are the meanings of the sacraments to which we appeal? From what is the gospel saving us? What is sin?

Shortly after I started organizing the presentation of these issues, I realized that it was essential to deal with the relationship between Christ and the believer. This is because the church is made up of men and women who testify to a personal faith in the Son of God and without whom the church would be meaningless. So, the structure of this book reflects the conviction that it is not possible to talk about the church if we do not talk about the personal relationship of its members with Christ and how this relationship is established through a particular tradition, that is, through those symbols and sacraments that give it shape and consistency. This is why the reader will find that the second section of this book is also a vision of the church, but a vision developed from the point of view of the relationship of the believer to Jesus, and their symbolic expressions.

Saltwater and Freshwater

These days there is a strong tendency to unify everything under a common denominator, say, the globalization of culture, economics, and science, combined in a strange way with an equally strong tendency toward individualism. The first is expressed through talk of regional markets, coordinated with development policies, and a tendency to overcome national borders through community relationships among nations. The second privileges hedonism and personal satisfaction as undisputed values. Both tendencies serve a third element particular to our time: conceptual ambiguity. Blessing and curse, comedy and tragedy, saltwater and freshwater; these coexist in conceptual ambiguity. There are undisputed values within the movement that consider the human community as one single entity, sharing one world. But this conception becomes dangerous when it is perceived as disregarding the specific characteristics of each nation and the positive value of the differences. It establishes a biased appraisal of each nation's cultural contributions and conceals the inequality and the evident unfairness of the distribution of resources and of access to welfare. There are also personal and individual values that should not be abandoned in relation to community identity, particularly those related to the rights and feelings of a person. In the end, we all come to the world as individual beings, separate from others, and we will leave it in the same way. But an excessive individualism that forgets that the other person also has rights and that his or her life is intimately linked to ours is also a distortion of human individuality.

We are called to be Christ's church in this particular cultural context. This book was written from a broader context. It accepts that what we call church is an entity created by the Holy Spirit, living with the juxtaposition of being both communal and a place where everyone has his own personal name. It is a place to meet and support each other, and also a place where silence and tears are respected with no explanations needed. The church is that entity that experiments within its own essence, perhaps as no other one; it is a dual movement: it puts together yet distinguishes, gathers under one Word yet respects and values the words of others. At the same time, and perhaps as a paradox, the church is that place where the message of God is clearly, but also faintly, heard. God's message can be clearly heard because there is the hope that in it, as in no other place, God will reign and will be recognized as a governing and driving force in our lives. Its strength originates in Christ and in his presence in the community. So too does its weakness because the church is the community of those who, though aware of this responsibility, are also aware of the distance between God's message and our partial and rudimentary expressions. It can be as faint as the weak voice of the crucified because God's Word is manifested and communicated through our limited words and strength. And it is this play between strength and weakness that should prevent the Christian church from being proud and from presenting itself as an example before the world. When it does so it becomes a caricature of the church Christ wished to establish; it is not His real and effective representative. We use the weak hands God gave us to share a powerful and transformative message. We announce it with our faint voice.

An Evangelical Theology

It is important to state from the very beginning that this book is a meditation about the church based on an *evangelical* theology. I do not mean to say that this theology is better than others, but, simple as it is, is thus the theology on which we base and develop our faith and testimony, and where I feel the biblical faith is expressed in a genuine way. It is from this point of view that I value other expressions of Christ's church and am convinced that someday the Holy Spirit will surprise all of us by fusing us into one body. While we continue using different denominational identities, it is not our task to oppose them, but to live out our faith genuinely where the Lord has planted us and be open so that His Word may transform and show us His ways. In this sense, I have been enriched from the experience of sharing in the heart of the Faith and Order Commission of the World Council of Churches, with brothers and sisters of the Roman Catholic Church and the Orthodox churches. Here we have gotten to know the point of view of one another and to discover how much we have in common within the different expressions of Christianity. We have also learned to note the real distances between us with respect to doctrine and to eschew the superficial

INTRODUCTION

and distortive ways in which the different positions have been introduced, an attitude that is so harmful to the testimony of believers.

Finally, I would like to state that I believe that the best thing that the church can offer to our contemporary society is to truly be the church. The temptation to want to do everything is always there, particularly in a world in need of so many vital things. Nevertheless, it happens that, while there are many important and necessary things that can be taken care of by other organizations, being the church and making its own unique contributions is something no one else will do for it. The task of being the church is perhaps the most delicate mission God has ever entrusted to human beings. This is true from the very moment when, inside the church, we are-with-others at the same time that we keep our individuality, and we are-with-God while we are called to remain faithful to our human essence. Once we are constituted as the church there is no other way to truly be the church than to share the gospel that has gathered us together.

I write as a minister of the Methodist Church who enjoys dialogue and exchange with brothers and sisters from very diverse ecclesiastical origins. Such plurality, while it complicates our faith, allows us to discover the conceptual and doctrinal richness of our churches, even as it clarifies those aspects where the different streams have not yet merged. For this reason, the reader will find that these pages do not just expose the ecclesiology in which we live out our faith, but also try to review our concepts and practices so that we can walk toward coming together, so that the differences can be understood as complementary information and not as elements that divide and exclude. The challenge of being a church transcends denominations and invites us to think with a broad perspective, which may go far beyond the territory we currently occupy. Consequently, I hope that these pages will contribute to all denominations being open to dialogue, helping us think about ourselves as Christ's church and as children of God, and to do so in the best way possible. We should not deny the world around us the experience of getting to know a community of people who believe that they have been rescued by God and who are willing to share that good news with everybody else.

PART 1: Being Church

1

People of God or Body of Christ?

The church is the community of men and women gathered by the Holy Spirit in order to express the will of God to the world. This condition and this mission constitute the being of the church. As we explore them we can appreciate that being the church is a wonderfully rich and deep experience.

We can say that the church is a place where a person can live out his or her faith, and also that the church is a community where the love of Christ should be shown to the people around us. Yet, the church is also a community for worshiping and studying the word of God, and the church is that place where we grow and find ourselves. When we think of the church we do not think of a building. We think of the people, all of whom are different from each other. In the church, different generations come together, different cultures and tastes get mingled. Traditions and styles, ways of talking and ideologies, different personal and social choices: they are all gathered together in the church. Taking all of these into account, we can adjust our first definition in order to arrive at a broader, although less precise, affirmation: the church is a space given by God. The aim of this chapter is to explore that space.

The Church as the People of God

As we proceed toward a deeper understanding of the church, we should take a look at two expressions we often use to refer to it. We say that the church is the people of God. In the Old Testament, the Israelites are addressed as "the people of God." They are the ones the Lord has chosen to communicate his word to the world. The concept of being the people of God was understood, from the very beginning, as something very exclusive and limited to the Israelites. Thus, it was thought that only those coming from that seed were truly part of "the people of God," while those who did not belong to the nation of Israel were not covered by His protection. However, this idea was questioned even in biblical times. The story told in the book of Ruth shows how a foreigner, Ruth, who was a Moabite and thus did not belong to "the people of God," could "discover" the real God and, by her own will, join the community of believers. This is not the only example in the Old Testament: there is a striking example in the book of Exodus. We are told that at the very moment the Hebrew people were about to leave for Egypt to be freed from slavery "a mixed crowd also went up with them" (Exod 12:38). Who were these people? The text does not need to explain this because the reader has no doubt that it refers to other people who were also slaves in Egypt, and when they saw God's liberating project they decided to join the cause. It is important to see that the text indicates that the Israelites had no trouble receiving them and that they were incorporated into the rest of the people of God right away. There is not a single narrative in Exodus referring to this crowd as a group separate from the rest of Israel. They became people of God from the moment they embraced the faith of Israel.

Later we encounter a second instance when belonging to the people of God was understood more as a responsibility than as a privilege. There has always been a group who has understood being part of "the people of God" as giving them privileges over the rest of humanity. They felt that God protected them in such a way that they could do what in fact they should not do, that is, take advantage of their neighbors. They thought this way: "If we are the people protected by God and He has chosen us, nothing bad will happen to us," and "any sin we may commit will in the end be forgiven by God, who loves us so much." They were only one step away from thinking that God *must* forgive us because we are his people. It is easy to fall into this trap. The prophets rose up against this attitude. They announced to Israel that being the people of God was a responsibility and not a privilege over other nations. If they failed in that responsibility they would face the Day of the Lord.

There are a series of images scattered in the prophetic books describing the Day of the Lord. "Day of the Lord" is an expression that refers to the day when God will gather all nations in order to judge them. While some were expecting that in that final day God would congratulate them for what a nice and fair people they had become, the prophets were there to remind them that, on that particular day, there would be more judgment than happiness for them.

> Alas for you who desire the day of the Lord!
> Why do you want the day of the Lord?
> It is darkness, not light . . .
>
> (Amos 5:18)

Amos does not say that the Day of the Lord will be only judgment and punishment. What is at stake is that those who feel protected because they belong to the people of God and live without openly expressing their faith in their lives will find out that God's plan is different. Yet the same prophet Amos says, "Seek me and live" (Amos 5:4). For God does not desire the sinner's death, but his conversion.

So, as time went by it was clear that being the people of God was not an ornament to be exhibited before the nations who did not belong to that category, but a responsibility to be exercised in the world. The mission of the people of God is to be a witness of the will of God for the whole creation before the nations. And the nations include those peoples who do not know Him.

By the time of the New Testament, this restrictive concept of the people of God was still alive even though it clashed with the ideas of the prophets and other biblical authors. The arrival of the Son of God was to produce such a drastic change in the faith of Israel that only a few were mature enough to understand it. Sometimes we misjudge the people who did not understand the message of Jesus in that time. However, we should remember that it must have been difficult to distinguish between the words of the real Son of God and the words of all the others who claimed to be the real Messiah. Besides, it is known that Jesus' message clashed with the message that the wise and illustrious took to be the message from the one sent by God. It helps us understand Jesus' words when He says, "I thank you, Father, Lord of heaven and earth, because you have hidden these from the wise and the intelligent and have revealed them to infants" (Matt 11:25). Or when the Apostle Paul tells us, "but God chose what is foolish in the world to shame the wise"(1 Cor 1:27).

This is not an approval of ignorance; nor is it a call to give up studying. It is a declaration that the wisdom of God has different coordinates than those expected by the wise in that time. The revolution of Jesus created a new perspective. The wisdom of the day became the darkness of ignorance because the new understanding of reality and the message of God was to come through the experience of the death and resurrection of Christ. Those who believed they knew everything found themselves to be empty-handed.

The Church as the Body of Christ

In this new situation created by the arrival of the Messiah and His message, the believers who gathered in the newly formed church considered themselves as forming "the body of Christ." This idea is expressed in many texts in the New Testament. Even though in the beginning it was the heir of the Jewish concept of the people of God as a community that should serve their fellows and be responsible for communicating God's message to all people, it also soon generated that distortion where they understood that being the church was a privilege that placed them above the rest of the people. Consider two texts. In 1 Cor 12:27 it is said, "Now you are the body of Christ and individually members of it." This statement is made within a broader context of a passage about the tasks that everyone is to develop in the dynamics of the church. Some are called to be teachers, others to be preachers, others to be healers, others to administrate and thus become "the body of Christ." This means that we should perform the role that was assigned to us in that body. The image of the body is excellent because we all know what happens when one part is not performing properly. Even if we do not know exactly where it is placed in our body and what its function is, if one part is not working, the whole body suffers and raises the alarm.

Hence being the body of Christ is an awesome responsibility and not a privilege. If we do not comply with our tasks, someone somewhere in the body will be injured. If we do not function properly, a fever or pain will stop the organism. So when we say that the church is the body of Christ we mean that each member has a unique task in God's plan, a task that cannot be transferred to others. Discovering this task is part of our responsibility.

The second text can be found in Eph 1:22–23: "And he has put all things under his feet and has made him the head over all things for the church, which is his body, the fullness of him who fills all in all." This is a beautiful text and it should be read within the whole passage in which it is located, but now let's pay attention to certain details. It is argued that Christ is the head of the church and then that the church is the body of Christ. This recurrent image in the New Testament leads to a major conclusion. It captures the relationship between Christ and His church, highlighting the fact that, Christ being the head, He is the one who governs and rules. Therefore the body cannot rebel against Him who is a crucial and irreplaceable organ and who allows the body to live and develop. Going a step further, we can observe that the body has life only if it is united with its head, so that if that link is severed there will be no future for any of its members.

When we say that the church is the body of Christ we mean this: it is Christ who rules. Christ is not any member of the body but the one who gives life to the rest of the body. It is fascinating to observe through history how human beings have managed to transform the power of God into our human power. With the passage of time, Christians took the expression "under his feet" not as a call for the church to serve Christ, but as a claim that the church be served by everything around it. Like those who misunderstood the concept of being God's people as a privilege and not as a service to the world, Christians took the idea that the church is "the body of Christ" to mean that the whole creation should pay homage to them. The text in Ephesians says otherwise: everything has been put under the feet of Christ and the church must have Him as its head. This means that the church must put itself under Christ, who will guide her conduct according to His will. It means that the church should have no other orientation than Christ's. If it does not, then it has put aside a fundamental aspect of its call. When the church is not serving God's plans and seeks to acquire privileges, it shows that it has given up an essential characteristic of its being. In a real way it has stopped "being church."

The church is the people of God and the body of Christ. It is neither God nor Christ. If the church forgets what it is and pretends to become another thing, it loses its identity and its credibility. This would not be the first time that the words of the church sound hollow because they are built upon human and earthly powers and not founded in the service of the gospel. On the other hand, one of the most significant experiences of the believer happens when he or she realizes that to be a Christian is to be part of a body that is much larger and broader than the congregation he or she attends regularly. The church transcends geographical and temporal boundaries; it runs from the origins of time and will survive when there is no memory of us. However, the church that will not be defeated is the church of Christ, the church that is a servant to the suffering and a companion to those who are alone. It is the church that resists the temptation of power and remains faithful to the message of peace and justice, of solidarity and humility, that will endure. If it ignores this, its message turns grey and tepid—and the Lord can tell what is genuine from what is spurious.

Nobody Can Be a Church in Our Place

To be the church is to have an irreplaceable identity. The really interesting thing about the church that makes it different from other social organizations is that its identity does not consist of a definition it gives itself, but in its relation to Christ. Christ is the identity of the church. It is not the other way around: the church is not Christ's identity. What do I mean? Consider two points.

First, the church is established by Christ's decision to be its Head. It is not our decision. *Technically*, we cannot establish a church because every church is created by Christ Himself through the work of the Holy Spirit. In this sense, the church cannot be said to be a human community since it expresses the presence of Christ among the people in that specific time and place. It is Christ who provides meaning and identity to the church. Without Him it loses all significance and reason for being.

Second, the church is effectively a human entity made up of people who run, organize, and lead it. The church is an organization that cannot claim that its spiritual and transcendent dimension frees it from mistakes or even sins. That is why I say that the church is not Christ. If it were, we would, on the one hand, put the blame on Christ for our mistakes and slip-ups. On the other hand, we would be confusing our thoughts with His. We must always remember that the Lord comes to us in his mercy and good will and not because we deserve it. As it is beautifully written in Eccl 5:2, "for God is in heaven, and you upon earth."

2

Being an Evangelical (and Catholic) Church

The Visible Church and the Invisible Church

Let us now look at the distinction between the visible and the invisible church. The visible church is the church we all can perceive, the church that identifies itself as such and introduces itself by means of its buildings, authorities, and members. It is the church that can be measured using sociological tools, that can be analyzed like any other human entity, that constitutes itself as an organization, and that develops its mission in a concrete and visible way. We can say it is the "institutional" church, with all the possibilities and limitations implied by such a condition. It is obvious that we cannot confuse it with the buildings we see in our neighborhoods. The building is the sanctuary, not the church. I mean here that the church is the community of people that can be observed and examined with all its virtues and defects. Considering that we are its members, no doubt we will find many things that could be done better.

There is another dimension to the church, that is, the invisibility of the church. The invisible church is the church of Christ, the one that is present whenever two or three gather in His name and that defines itself in such a way that it cannot be reduced to a mere human expression. The Holy Spirit works according to its own free will and cannot be shaped or locked into our tastes, models, and thoughts. It is not limited to buildings, cultures, denominations, languages or any of our human barriers. The church of Christ is there, where the Holy Spirit is. It is also the church that has existed through the past centuries, the church of those who have preceded us on the path of faith and who have offered their testimonies, brothers and sisters to whom we are linked through our belonging to the people of God. The invisible church is the church that is not present even if we are standing in the most prestigious cathedral in the city, or next to the most well-known preacher, if God does not approve the work that is being done in that place. The invisible church is the "actual" church, the one that is not based on our abilities—rather, it exists despite our behavior and *in*abilities—but on the free and generous grace of God.

One of the most routine, and least perceived, miracles is that God grants us His invisible presence in the visible church made up of men and women. By this we mean that the invisible church is present in the world through the visible church. When the church preaches, educates, creates links among people, and shares the faith and the sacraments, among other things, it is making visible a deeper reality that is invisible and transcends what we do. We may say that the task of each member is to make visible that dimension of the presence of God that is and will be invisible to our eyes.

Here are some considerations that will help us better understand the nature of the church:

1. This double dimension of the church (being visible and invisible) is a statement of our faith. We have to take into account that, for those who are outside, the only church that can be perceived is the visible one; consequently they will assess the church for its visible behavior. A common mistake is to accuse those who point out the mistakes of the church as "not understanding" or "of not accepting the church or the gospel." It is true that a correct understanding of the deep and invisible dimensions of what the church is should be done from within the faith itself and that, without this faith, it is not possible to perceive the final dimension of God's project for it. But it is unfair to demand that those objectively examining what is going on in the church adhere to our faith, and to conclude that a critic cannot be right. There is no doubt that when a church is criticized in good faith, this helps it grow and improve. Christians should receive and carefully analyze the claims of critics. Moreover, critics coming from different perspectives, or with other intentions, will help us understand how we are perceived. They

can help us see that those things we may believe to be right and fair are not so.

2. In light of what I said above, we should acknowledge that God does not give his church a blank check to be filled in according to its will. The invisible church of Christ manifests itself freely in the church made up of people, provided that it fulfills its call and remains faithful to its foundation, that is, the gospel. When the church puts aside the gospel, it may physically look like the church, but it is nothing more than a hollow shell. The church should always be under Christ and not above Him. If it pretends to dominate over Christ and twist His words, it will not only lose its identity as the church, but it will also not be the genuine and noble community that God wants.

3. The church must be the vehicle that expresses the voice of the gospel. In this sense, when expressing itself, the church must carefully choose its words. On the one hand, since these will be received as the voice of Christ on earth, they should be carefully chosen. On the other hand, the church must be both humble and firm when speaking because what is at stake is the invisible credibility of God expressed through his visible church.

It scarcely needs saying that every time a particular church is involved in an act of corruption, an offense, or an attack against a person's dignity, the whole church is injured. This is so because the visible church is perceived as the only real church. It is fine if, after receiving these blows, the church is purified of error and the true church, wherever it is, shines with more brilliance. One of the most embarrassing situations is that of the church hiding its crimes "so as not to damage the image of the church." We may ask ourselves, if the church cannot hide its sins from God, from whom do believers think they are hiding their sins?

Being an Evangelical and Catholic Church

When we read documents coming from different churches, we can see readily that the Catholic Church refers to itself and considers itself to be "*the* church." By contrast, evangelical churches express themselves as "being part of the church." Both ways reflect not just how the different churches understand themselves but also how they understand their relationship with other churches.

The Catholic way, a way shared with the Orthodox churches, gives priority to the sense of the catholicity of the church as expressed in the Apostles' Creed. It has no trouble stating that it is *the* church of Christ. This idea implies a negative judgment on the rest of the Christian churches; they are considered incomplete, separate communities of faith but not churches strictly speaking. Over time that way of thinking has become more and more a conceptual issue. Today it can be understood to mean that the church is always the whole church, undivided. However, in this tradition we can still sense some aftertaste of exclusivity, the notion that "other" Christians come up short in regard to salvation. This is reinforced by the statement of apostolic succession as a criterion for the validity and continuity of the faith, and by the claim to authority due to the historic church in Rome existing from the very beginning of the primitive church.

The evangelical churches, also known as Protestant churches, understand themselves to be a *portion* of the church of Christ. They acknowledge that there are other, distinct churches with diverse traditions and customs, with theological aspects that distinguish one from another, but that the differences are not serious enough to exclude them from the larger church of Christ. The evangelical churches prioritize the continuity of the testimony of believers and the proclamation of the gospel through time as granted by the Holy Spirit, who raises witnesses wherever it wills. Though we usually refer to the evangelical churches as "not having an apostolic succession," it is necessary to examine this expression because it reduces such succession to a chain of individuals, whereas the church should be interested in the succession of the apostolic *faith*. As such, the apostolic succession, as understood by the Catholic and Orthodox churches, is not perceived as a valid criterion of apostolicity, since the criterion can be manipulated by purported "acts of the Holy Spirit" if it is mechanically linked to human decisions that reflect human interests in most cases. Within this model, the chain of faith becomes a physical and human chain, yet its own story shows that many of its links were not worthy enough to transmit, convey, or be representative of Christ. That is the reason why evangelical churches acknowledge the historical succession of the Spirit of God in the genuine proclamation of the Word of God and find the expression "being *part* of the church" a much better way of speaking. It does justice to the inclusiveness of the Spirit that goes beyond our human realizations.

BEING AN EVANGELICAL (AND CATHOLIC) CHURCH

Let us stop for a moment and examine both concepts. It is obvious that both formulations can claim historical basis and ancient theologies, as they readily do. Moreover, if we go deep into the texts of the New Testament we will also come across texts to pull water to our own mill, depending on where we look and how we interpret them. We believe that in both positions there are valuable elements as well as elements that should be mitigated. On the one hand, the statement "we are the church," as the Catholic Church says, should give an account of the meaning of being "the" church of Christ in relation to all the other churches around the world that are preaching the gospel, baptizing, and celebrating the Lord's Supper and that have their own martyrs of the faith. Is it possible to be the true Christian church and not recognize that other compelling ecclesial reality that lives and expresses its faith outside of the Roman Catholic community? When the Catholic Church asserts that those churches that are not Catholic are deficent in regard to salvation because they are separate from Rome, in fact what is evident is a failing in the Catholic Church to discern the action of the Holy Spirit beyond itself and within the spaces it cannot control. Thus, it reveals that it is closed to that portion of God's action and it places itself at the margin of much of what God is promoting in the world today.

The evangelical churches consider themselves "one part" of the church. This fragmentation has its own problems because Jesus' will (and He has explicitly prayed for this) was "that they may all be one": "As you, Father, are in me and I am in you, may they also be in us, so that the world may believe that you have sent me" (John 17:21). As evangelical churches, we have been taking things much too lightly, not considering that what is at stake in speaking of the unity of the church is the conversion of the world. If we are merely "a portion" we are in breach of the law, at least when confronted with the explicit will of the Lord as expressed on the day when He looked up to heaven and said so. The biblical testimony is clear: the unity of the church is something that God desires, while the differences should always be understood as a product of human rebelliousness. In the language I am using here we should say that the invisible church is the united church, while the visible church is the one that is divided. In a real sense it is looking for its full identity in Christ. Thus, what evangelical churches should show is how Christ's will for only one church is expressed through their mission and ministry. How this catholicity (universality) of the church is expressed in its life and message when living separated from other churches seems to be the standard way of living out faith.

The importance of this issue has not been sufficiently explored from the point of view of the evangelical faith. Our origins as "national" churches in Europe or as "dissenting" churches, struggling for the practice of the faith in hostile environments, have prevented us from considering this weakness in our witness. We were born as churches that needed to differentiate ourselves from the rest of Christianity, and this has imparted to us a characteristic that we should examine critically so that it does not end up being a burden. Too often evangelicals have described themselves as if the evangelical churches had a certain "ecclesiological shortage." This prevents them from appreciating themselves as being part of something broader. Yet, I believe such shortage is not essential but practical and should be overcome, not through changing the understanding of the church, but by exploring the universal dimension of our identity as a church. It is crucial that evangelical churches should understand that when they invite somebody into the Christian faith, to convert them to Christ, they are not inviting her or him to join a certain portion of the church, but to join the undivided church whose Head is Christ. We invite the world to the totality and fullness of Christ, not to a portion of it, because Christ is not divided. In this sense, each church, each denomination, is the "actual" church of Christ, which does not mean that the rest of the churches are not.

From this point of view it becomes necessary to consider the fact that the evangelical churches are also catholic from the moment they are part of the reality of being the one, holy, catholic and apostolic church of Christ on earth. We affirm that every time we recite the Nicene Creed we acknowledge in it an ancestral and genuine formulation of faith in the Lord.

The Unity of the Church of Christ

Everything mentioned just now does not mean we should leave aside our points of view and denominational identities and gather as soon as possible with whoever wants to join us. This would mean we are not taking seriously the faith we support and that gives significance to our own and our predecessors' witness. While the Spirit does not unite all churches into one, the church will go on using denominational identities for its own purpose, and our task is not to oppose this but to be open to what it might offer. In any case, the path toward unity is a project of the Holy Spirit, who will indicate the right time and correct wording.

Also, we should note that it is false to say that all the divisions within the church are the consequence of human sin. What should be primary in the church's witness is faithfulness to the word of God and, though this includes a call toward the unity of the church, it is not correct to claim that such unity is a final criterion to which everything else should be subject. Reality shows that on occasion what has been at stake has been faithfulness to God's project. In order to be faithful to that call there was a division in the visible church that allowed preaching the word to continue through an alternate route. We cannot sharply assert that each and every division of the church in the past has been produced by sin. We should consider that in certain circumstances it was an act of God. Experience teaches us that when the visible church stops reflecting the invisible church, the Holy Spirit finds alternative ways to express itself.

On the other hand, the movement toward unity reaches further than the unity of the churches, since its aim is the encounter of all humanity (we might say of the whole creation) with God. Within this plan of God, the church is a provisional and instrumental entity depending on His major project. In the fullness of the ages the church will cease to be; it will be like the seed in fertile soil, which disappears to reveal an infinite, richer reality. The church is at the threshold of a tremendous act of God and is living its faith expecting this reality to become effective in the fullness of the ages. While waiting for a deeper renovation, it must never stop relating to Christ as the One who assures that the whole process will lead to the integration of humankind into a permanent and definite unity.

This provisional character of the church must not be confused with what has been called the "ecclesiological deficit" of the evangelical churches, that is, the limitations of the churches to perceive their own lack of belonging to the universal community. On the contrary, to accept the instrumental character of the church regarding the project of God strengthens its ecclesiology since it prevents it from seeing it is as an end in itself, and provides it with a base where it can consolidate its identity as a church in process. It can begin to see itself as a community that, though still a preview of the new creation, acknowledges its own incompleteness and hopes to be transformed once again. The church should always look outside because it senses that it is becoming a place for the salvation of the world. If it looks inside, it will not find anything beneficial or significant for its mission in the world. The Scriptures and the reality where they should be applied are external entities, and as such they possess features the church has to make an effort to address. Each individual who draws near to the church looking for answers to his or her questions is an "external" entity who, precisely because of this, will question the reality of the church he or she is approaching. And, in doing so, he or she will help the church grow.

3

Is the Church a Perfect Institution? (Am I Perfect?)

In the previous chapter I made a distinction between the visible and the invisible church. I highlighted the fact that the invisible church can be identified by the action and presence of the Holy Spirit, which may or may not be present in the visible church. In this chapter I will consider the visible church, the one formed every time we gather in Christ's name, the one organized to perform the mission the Lord has entrusted to us.

A Very Common Mistake: The Church Does Not Sin

One of the most common mistakes of Christians is to say that the church does not sin, that the church cannot be corrupted, and that those who make mistakes and commit wrongs are "the children of the church" and not the church itself. Consequently, the church remains flawless before God. In general, this kind of defense of the church is constructed on the argument that the church is the body of Christ and, therefore, Christ can neither sin nor be responsible for our mistakes. This reasoning seems precise and logical, but it is not convincing. Every time we hear an argument like this in defense of the church we feel there is something artificial in the reasoning. Again, this argument is not convincing. What is wrong with it?

To answer this question we need to revisit the biblical image of the church as the body of Christ. It is interesting to discover in 1 Corinthians how clearly this idea is expressed (see also Rom 12:4–8; 1 Cor 6:15; 12:12–17). To speak of the body of Christ is not another way to refer to Jesus; it is a way to mark the activities and testimony of the believers. In other words, the image of "being the body of Christ" is not used to apply the virtues of God to Christians; it is a call to them to become accountable for preaching the gospel. If they do not comply with this, the mission of Christ is weakened. Christians are the body of Christ in the sense that they constitute the community through which God wants His message to be spread and salvation abound. Note that 1 Cor 6:15 deals with the responsible use of the body, a warning made in the context of a society with a high level of sexual promiscuity and all kinds of excesses. The question "Do you not know that your bodies are members of Christ?" is asked in the context of rejecting prostitution (v. 16) and should be understood in such a way. Each believer should consider that whatever he does with his body directly affects his relationship with Christ. The message is this: being united with Christ should lead us to examine our lives and inhibit us from harming our bodies. When we harm our bodies, we harm the relationship with the One who is the Lord of life, and life includes the body. This is confirmed in verse 19 where it says that "your body is a temple of the Holy Spirit," which in context means that because we have been purchased by God, our bodies do not belong to us exclusively. Whatever we do with our bodies affects our bond with God.

In 1 Cor 12:27 "being the body of Christ" is the image used to explain the dynamics of the church and its relationship with God. Each believer is a member of the body and has a specific function in God's plan. In this case, being the body of Christ means being a part of that body and an essential element whose absence weakens the whole structure and causes it to stop functioning properly. Thus, the image seeks to make the believer conscious of the delicate responsibility she or he has from the moment she or he accepts the faith and becomes a member of a body larger than herself or himself. Believers benefit from such integration and, as a consequence, it requires them to take into account the rest of the body. Being a member of the church links believers with brothers and sisters they do not know, who embrace the same faith in contexts and situations different from theirs. At the same time, a member of the church assumes responsibilities that come from the very relationship with Christ, from his testimony and his preaching, which happily have been fruitful in the life of the believer. To forget this leaves our faith unsupported and puts our membership in the body of

Christ in a terminal crisis. Plainly and simply: we stop being the body of Christ.

Returning to our starting point, it is not convincing to say, "The church makes no mistakes, its children do." When we speak like this we confuse the body of Christ with Christ Himself, a confusion produced on two levels. The first is that, according to the use of the expression in Paul's epistle, "being the body of Christ" is an image and not a doctrinal statement. It does not say that the gathering of believers is a sacrament of the resurrected Christ. It uses this literary image as a sublime example of the relationship between the believers within the church and the relationship of each and all of them with the Christ living in them.

The second level of confusion results from the failure to distinguish Christ from the church that preaches Him. And it is interesting to note that the image of the human body as a picture of the relationship between believers and with Christ in the church can also help us understand the problem. The bond between the body we inhabit and what we are is very subtle; sometimes it is very difficult to distinguish ourselves from our bodies. The carrot we have just eaten has gone into us, and is part of us, but we do not say or feel that we are that carrot. If we lose a hand or suffer a loss of hearing, our whole self will be affected, and not only our body; but we do not stop being because of such a situation, neither are we "less" because of this handicap. I am this body, but at the same time I am more than my body. Likewise, the church's being "the body of Christ" manifests an intimate and close relationship with Him, but it should not be understood as assimilation to Christ Himself or to His qualities. Consider the wisdom of the gospels once again in Matt 18:20: "For where two or three are gathered in my name, I am there among them." It is clear that the text in no way implies that Christ *is* the people gathered (the church); He is announced as a different presence that joins those gathered under His name.

That the church is the body of Christ calls the church to responsibility before the "owner" of that body; it does not establish any kind of privilege to excuse the church from the sinful passions of those who constitute it.

The Daily Church

Another aspect that we should keep in mind in this brief survey of the church as the body of Christ is that the body is always visible. To say that things and persons are "easy on the eyes" is more than a witty phrase; it expresses a deep truth of our existence: we establish relations with each other through our bodies. Thus, the church will be judged by what it shows and not by what it conceals; it will be judged based on what it offers as a visible and specific church and not because of any other theological or spiritual reality we might create. The curious thing about this condition of being assessed for what is visible—which might seem limited and even unfair to some people—is that this is something that God not only wishes but has actually established Himself.

One of the main reasons for the church's existence is the people who are on its fringes. Had the Lord not established a mission toward the world, that is, "outside" the church, it would not have been necessary, at least not the church as we know it from the stories in the book of Acts. The church could have been a community of initiates who rejoiced together in the revealed faith and in their calling to share what they experienced when walking with Jesus; they could have gathered to celebrate these memories with no relation to what might be going on outside their own circle. But it was not so, and there was not only a call to obey, but also a mission to execute.

In this context, every congregation in its specific neighborhood is to call everybody to the faith and preach the gospel of salvation, but those who are invited to join the church watch it "from outside"; they receive the Word from believers whom they can see and observe objectively, from people who are in that sanctuary and preaching with their own words and living along the lines of a specific message. This view of the church from the outside is not a limited or anomalous situation of the mission. On the contrary, it is the natural, missionary context where the church has been placed. God knows that this is the situation where the testimony of His word is at stake and, in spite of it all, He has designed things this way. It is not my intention to limit the Holy Spirit, who acts according to its own will, and in general pleasantly surprises us, but experience shows that we come to faith and to the church through the action of the visible church, though this is not the only way.

What does this suggest in regard to the nature of the visible church? Let's examine three main consequences.

First, we should say that while the church offers salvation, it is also distinct from salvation. The daily, visible church bears the responsibility of being the sign and instrument of God's salvation. Let's make this point clear. The church does not save. Neither does it have a monopoly on salvation—just as an excellent sermon or the reading of the word wisely chosen does not save. He who saves is Christ, and that power cannot be delegated. While the church has the delicate task of bearing witness to God's action in history and testifying to the people of the grace given through the sacraments—the means of salvation—the church is not itself salvation.

At times, the church has believed itself to be the owner of those means and, consequently, has seen itself as the custodian of salvation. This happens when the means are confused with the end, that is, salvation. The church has been given the authority to identify the means of salvation and make known the abundant grace that God offers to human beings, but not salvation itself. Salvation belongs to God and transcends all possibility of human manipulation.

Second, this condition of the visible church—of being sign and instrument of salvation—bestows a higher value to its task and existence. It is not right to say that the real church is the invisible church and that the visible church is only a shadow of it. What we do in the life of the church is valuable within the purposes of God; and it is not a mere careless, human exercise that later will be written by the Lord Himself with beautiful capital letters if He agrees.

Hence, what the believer does is fundamental to the plan of salvation and should be taken with the utmost seriousness. No doubt God will reject everything that, though done in His name and invoking His presence, does not correspond with His will or His word. Yet, for those who are outside the church, those for whom the church has been established, that ordinary and earthly word is the only one that has been given to the church as testimony of the gospel.

Third, this vision gives to the visible church a function that, at least for the church, cannot be delegated: being a church. The Lord can make the stones shout out if necessary, but He gave us the responsibility of being the community who offers His word to those who do not know about Him. Of course, He can use other ways, and in fact He does so daily when our way is blocked because of our own shortcomings and weaknesses or, simply, because it is a way to remind us that we are not the only ones who know Him, nor are we His exclusive representatives. Far from considering that those other ways might become an excuse for our weaknesses, the mission that has been given to the church is a task that no other community will take on in its place.

Us and the Church

Some people leave the church because they find it is not committed enough to resolving conflicts in society or to working for causes that make for a more humane world. Other people, from the opposite direction, leave because they consider it not spiritual enough. At times, some people find the church too indulgent toward injustice, while other people find it too committed to social work, and still others focus on the mistakes, or even the crimes, that took place in its long life. When we look objectively into the history of the medieval church, loaded with corruption and human power; when we see the cross and the sword in the conquest and the subjection of peoples in the Americas; when we observe the role played by the majority of German Christians during the Nazi era, we cannot avoid turning the classic question "Is there salvation outside the church?" on its head and asking ourselves if there is salvation *within* the church. The church should listen carefully to this questioning and acknowledge that in most cases it is motivated by sincere critics of real events in the church's life and its historical development. Denying history or trying to justify the evil the church has done will only weaken its testimony and distance it from the people it was sent to serve. When this happens, the church gets in the way of the gospel's being proclaimed, and it separates the people from Christ instead of being a place where God's Word is offered to all. A lot of people feel alienated from the church and so leave it, looking elsewhere for what they should have found there.

Saying all this does not release us from the responsibility to acknowledge that if we are the church and if, from an evangelical point of view, there is no other visible church than the one we form and bear responsibility for, we cannot demand from the church more saintliness than we are willing to contribute with our own testimony. Walking out of the church because we do not agree with its decisions is not the wise way to change it and help it improve. When we walk out we are taking those members away from the community who could, in our opinion, lead it to put ministry in action in more mature ways. Getting involved in social projects in order to change society should not be carried out at the expense of acknowledging the transcendent character of the mission of the church. On the contrary, the strength of the gospel expressed by the church should foster social justice and the commitment to work for a fair society. If we love the church, we must try to enrich it with such action. The church needs brothers and sisters who can see further than their own limitations and contribute to its development so that the visible church, the ordinary church, is closer to those for whom it has been created.

4

The Bible: Is It the Word of God?

Evangelical churches found their faith and their doctrine on the Bible. We say that our faith is biblical; when we want to confirm a statement we say that such and such a statement is biblical; sometimes we say "it is not biblical" if we want to cast a shadow on a statement's credibility. This issue is critical for the church, because the church is constituted under the authority of Scripture and not above it. Though it is true that the church decided which texts belong in the Bible and which do not (a task that has caused a lot of trouble throughout the history of Christianity), this does not mean that the church can act as if it were the owner of the Bible and, hence, not under its judgment. There is a hint of omnipotence when we say that the Bible "was given into the custody of the church" and for this reason the church acts as an authority over it. In fact, the church should serve the word and accept that it is used by the Spirit beyond its limits and beyond what we can imagine. In this way, the church is judged by Scripture and called through it to constant renewal and to look to God for direction in its mission.

This confidence in the Bible as a privileged source of doctrine and direction is a distinctive evangelical commitment that we should preserve; we should consider it one of the most valuable points within our ecclesial tradition. Nevertheless, it is necessary to adjust some of its principles in order to be able to continue standing by it as a principle for the church.

At the time of the Reformation in the sixteenth century, the age that gave birth to the Protestant and evangelical movement, this principle was called *sola scriptura* ("Scripture alone"). The Christian might look for orientation and inspiration in different places and systems, but the final criterion that would underwrite the veracity of any statement would be its coherence with Scripture. In the beginning this principle may have seemed easy to apply, but once we start going through the Bible's pages we realize it cannot be applied directly and literally. In the Bible there are lots of complex and obscure passages. In the Old Testament there are several statements that are difficult to reconcile with the love of God, not to mention with Jesus' testimony. What should be done with those passages that call us to wage war and violence? What should be done with those psalms that celebrate the misfortunes of enemies? How should we understand those texts concerning innocents murdered by the action of God, or during the conquest of Canaan, where the people living in the land before the Israelites arrived were literally expelled and deprived of their legitimate homeland? It is no easier in the New Testament, in which there is not a single, explicit condemnation of slavery or of polygamy, and in which we read that women should remain quiet in church and submit to their husbands. This and so many other passages are also the "word of God," and a church that says it privileges such a word should know how to read and interpret it.

The Bible *Is* the Word of God—or Does It *Contain* the Word of God?

In order to go deeper in this discussion, let us consider the difference between these two statements: the Bible *is* the word of God and the Bible *contains* the word. To say that the Bible is the Word of God presumes a direct and mechanical relationship between what it says and the message it tries to convey. We may ask how this relationship should be considered from the social and cultural context within which it was written, the place of the human author who wrote those stories and poems, and the religious conception of the world in which those lines were written. If every word and text is the direct word of God, how do we understand the relationship between the different parts of the same Scripture? How can we explain that Christians do not keep Sabbath in spite of the fact that the Bible commands it dozens of times and Jesus practiced it? How can we reconcile the story of the origins of the earth and of human beings with the scientific evidence that supports a very different understanding of those origins? We can go on asking such questions indefinitely.

Clearly, one alternative is to consider that the Bible contains the word of God. If so, then it is not necessary to read every line as if it were the divine word; rather, we may assume that the word of God is contained in the stories, oracles, letters, and prayers. The word comes together with a number of things that are not technically His word. In this way, we acknowledge that the Bible is a work inspired by God, but that it is not identified in every detail with His Word. It is understood that the biblical authors stamped their human characteristics on the text. The word of God comes to us inside a container, if you will, which is not part of it, and we should learn to distinguish the one from the other. For instance, the psalmist ends the beautiful Psalm 137 this way:

> O daughter Babylon, you devastator!
> Happy shall they be who pay you back
> what you have done to us!
> Happy shall they be who take your little ones
> and dash them against the rock!

The hate and thirst for revenge of the people whose children were murdered and whose rights were abolished can be clearly perceived. The psalmist allows his desire for revenge to get out of hand and shows this in his wish that the people of Babylon would suffer the same fate as the Israelites, or worse. We recognize this text as part of the Bible, but we cannot assume that it is the will of God for people and children. Take another example, this time from the New Testament:

> For the Lord's sake accept the authority of every human institution, whether of the emperor as supreme, or of governors. (1 Pet 2:13–14)

This text makes sense in the specific situation of the readers of Peter's first epistle, a moment when Christianity was spreading and its leaders wanted to avoid conflict with the Roman political authorities. If understood this way, it is the Word of God. But it cannot be understood as if it were the will of God for every time and context. What can be said of the oppressive regimes, dictatorships, and systems that conduct an organized violation of human rights and disregard the value of life? What can be said of corrupt authorities that impose themselves against people's will? What can be done when the authorities ban the church, so that it cannot preach or gather for worship? No doubt we can affirm that God does not want the believer to submit himself to illegitimate or oppressive authorities, *but that is what the biblical text says literally.*

To say that the Bible contains the word of God allows us to understand all the other texts that need to be considered from a contextual point of view so as to avoid making God say what He did not mean to say, which happens when we read Scripture literally and apply it in a mechanical way. We need to go deeper into Scripture, because if it contains the Word but is not completely identified with it, we may ask ourselves the question, to what extent is it the Word of God and to what extent is it a mere human word?

And the Word Became Literature

It is interesting to note that we often refer to the phrase "the Word became flesh" (John 1:14). From a theological point of view we have no trouble acknowledging this relationship between God and His human expression in Christ. We might not understand it fully, and even ask ourselves which is the correct way to understand its meaning, but we know it is part of the Christian faith from its beginnings and we accept it as a part of the formulation of the faith. The immediate consequence of the incarnation of God in Christ is that, through this action, God assumes human limitations. In Jesus of Nazareth, God assumes a certain geography (Palestine), a point in time (the first century CE), a people (Israel), a gender (masculine), and a language (Aramaic). None of these characteristics imply a higher status over other possibilities. In other words, Palestine was not a better place for God to be present than any other region on the planet, nor was the first century a more appropriate one in which to deliver the gospel to humanity than another period in time. Nor do we say that the people of Israel were better or that the masculine should prevail over the feminine. The Aramaic language spoken by Jesus was not better than other languages. In fact, it became obsolete and disappeared. However, those specific characteristics of human culture were constitutive of the incarnation of God in Christ. They were not mere accidents. That is to say, without them Jesus would not have been Jesus or the son of God. As is stated in the Epistle to the Philippians (2:6–7), "who, though he was in the form of God, did not regard equality with God as something to be exploited, but emptied himself, taking the form of a slave, being born in human likeness."

In Christ, God leaves aside "the shape" of God (who is not limited by time and place, social and cultural expressions, the need of a physical body, and the like) and, divesting Himself from those privileges, becomes human (i.e., he assumed human, cultural, political, and personal limitations). Is it possible to understand the relationship between God and His word by this analogy?

The analogy between the incarnation of Jesus of Nazareth and the incarnation in Scripture does indeed help us better understand our relationship with the biblical text. In the Scripture we find that the message of God, in order to become understood by human beings, accepted the limitations of our language. As God revealed Himself in Jesus, He reveals Himself in the written word. Consequently, the human "aspects" of that literary work (the context, the literary genre, each author's specific style, social and cultural influences) are not "mere" human aspects printed in the text, but fundamental elements essential to the human language that God employed to communicate in a way that we could understand.

We must not think that God would seek to use a "heavenly" language (for nobody would understand), or a text "sterilized" of all human contamination (because God does not reject the human element, but makes a profound use of it), or a word "purified" of human ideologies and passions (because it would be boring or obscure). On the contrary, God decided that the human dimension of His word had to remain a part of it, just as a specific eye color, a certain physical stature, and a particular language remained in Jesus. This did not mean these characteristics became normative or "holy." This way we can understand that those things that seem not to express the will of God in the Scriptures (murders, violence, injustice, unequal social relationships, etc.) are His word. They are not a shortcoming or defect, but a testimony of the humanity accepted by God in order to better communicate with us. The human aspect of Scripture—and here we include the ideologies inherent in the text, the meanness of some characters, the obscurity of some passages, etc.—is part of God's "taking the form of a servant" that expresses God's deep commitment to all that it means to be human. Becoming human led Him to the cross; becoming a written, human word—that is, literature—led Him to risk being misinterpreted. But, in any case, the general view is that the will of God is to commit Himself to humans, even putting His own credibility at stake. It might have been easier for Him to adopt a divine discourse (that is, not human), but had that been the case we would not recognize Him as the God of the Bible. He would be alone in His heaven, and we would be alone on the earth.

It is necessary to point out two final issues. It has been highlighted that Jesus' divinity was not evident. In other words, seeing Jesus was not enough to make one realize that He was the Messiah, the son of God. If it had been enough, the Roman soldiers would not have dared to torment him and nail him to the cross. Had Jesus' divinity been evident, who could have rejected his presence? Or if Jesus had exuded an undeniable aura that marked Him as the true son of God, how could we explain the disciples' doubts? It was necessary to see through the eyes of faith in order to discover in that body the divine and transcendent dimension. At the same time, neither is the character of the word of God evident in the biblical texts, since they should be read with eyes of faith in order to discover their divine message. Without this perspective, we can perceive their literary value, their beauty and historical import, but not their message. Also, the Bible constitutes a historical record of past events that is invaluable for the historian and the sociologist who studies former times, though its status as the word of God is perceived when we read it with the eyes of faith.

The second issue is that the analogy we introduced has certain limits. God was indivisible from Christ and in such a way that no distance could be perceived. Jesus was "truly God and truly man," according to the statement of the Council of Chalcedon, accepted by Christianity as a faithful expression of its faith. Consequently, the incarnation of Christ is a unique act, with no distance between the two natures. Thus, the presence of God among human beings is fully expressed in our time when Christ is present where "two or three come together in His name." The Bible is not a second incarnation but a privileged testimony without being God itself. It is true that it is an instrument chosen and given by God—given by Him as a means to know Him and not as an end in itself. Every approach to the word of God should be considered a means leading us to the knowledge of Christ; it must be an exploratory experience in which we ask, "Who is the God we believe in, where is the place He assigns us in His plan of salvation, and how do we relate with Him and our fellow man?"

The Church and the Word

We have pointed out that the church is formed under the authority of Scripture. We may now ask ourselves how this authority is put into action in the life of the church. There is some risk in believing that everything depends on how the church interprets the Scriptures, as if it could adapt the message to its own needs and liking. It is clear that the Scriptures must be interpreted by the church, but still the problem remains, because who can assure a correct interpretation? And experience shows that each time church authorities have tried to develop a normative interpretation for the church they fell prey to rigid and exclusive thinking that stifled the meaning of Scripture instead of letting Scripture speak for itself.

Our opinion is that we should understand Scripture's value for the function it performs in the life of the church and not because it might possess some kind of particular power. The Bible is not a talisman or a magical story. When read in the absence of faith, it is only a beautiful antique book with literary values we can appreciate, but as long as God uses it as His instrument to communicate the message, it transforms itself into the word of God. It is the use that God Himself gives Scripture that adds value and meaning beyond its own words. When God uses Scripture as a means to spark faith and give it content—or to correct the church, its mistakes and detours—this antique book becomes the living Word of God. It is through the action of the Spirit that this collection of stories, poems, and prayers is transformed into the word that God intends for each believer and for the world, going beyond the natural limitations of the human dimension that formed it and becoming the privileged message meant to reach everybody. It is the miracle of personal faith or of the renewed church that, coming from its reading, reveals it as the sacred Scripture, as the word of God for us.

5

A Church without Spirituality?

The church is founded in Christ and is guided by His Spirit. Christ is at the center of the church's life and gives it meaning. We raise our prayers to Him and we are always waiting for his guidance, his light to illuminate the winding roads of life and mission. This is our faith, upon which we found our life as believers and our involvement in the congregation. These statements that express the "spiritual base" of the church's life will surely be shared by most believers, beyond the subtle differences that each church will highlight in its own doctrine. Now, what we would like to explore in these pages is how such conviction translates into *our* spirituality. We do this because we understand that it is crucial for the mission of the church and because it is one of those aspects of the life of faith that, if not addressed, will impede our witness before a society that needs to rethink its aims and ask for a clear message. Anyway, we want to put forward an answer: there is no Christian church without spirituality. But what are we talking about?

Describing spirituality is a difficult task. Every time we try to do this, we step into the difficulties of our own rational language and its tendency to turn those things that are difficult to understand into something concrete. At the same time, it is also difficult to describe how spirituality works in the life of the believer. For instance, we may have various understandings of the doctrine of the Trinity or of the extent to which God acts in history. This will not necessarily be reflected in the external aspects of our Christian life; moreover, it is quite possible that if nobody ever asks about it, it is not possible to tell the difference between those who have a different opinion on any of these issues. Something similar may happen if we could place upon the scale our understanding of life and death, eternal life, or the way God rules our life, and we could contrast that against the experience of others from our own congregation. Probably we will be surprised to find out how many different ways of understanding the faith exist within the same community. The paradox is that, when we are referring to spirituality, those things "that cannot be seen" happen to be the most visible and evident in people's lives. The different attitudes as to what we consider "spiritual" modify the way we live our faith internally, and also in every exterior aspect. For example, let's analyze the following situations:

a) We pray as an activity of the community, which makes sense as far as it shares our feelings, requests, and wishes for the church, or we consider prayer an activity that mainly expresses a personal relationship with God. Do we understand that they are mutually exclusive or that both of them should complement each other?

b) We see in the presence of a poor person, marginalized from the economic and social system, somebody who deserves our help for reasons of ethics and human solidarity; or beyond that, we find in him or her the spiritual presence of Christ Himself, who chose to become one of them and who appears to us through this person.

c) Do we consider that the Holy Spirit manifests itself in a visible way through particular situations as the gift of speaking in tongues or a healing miracle, or do we believe that its acts are invisible and we do not believe that it manifests itself through actions? Do we reject any of these views—in favor of one of them—or do we accept both, or consider another possibility?

By assuming any of these theological attitudes, people become members of or leave a certain church. Consider a congregation of true believers, persons possessing a mature faith, or who think they are influenced by some doctrine that leads them away from a strong faith, maybe too liberal and skeptical or perhaps too spiritual and naïve.

Are Spirit and Matter Opposed?

What we call spirituality is one of those dimensions which cannot be measured and, different from the external actions of human beings, they originate on one's inside and they resist being classified, labeled, and transformed into numbers. If we do so, we will possibly feel that we are inadequate tools for the matter we are dealing with. From the very beginning we can see difficulties arise in several fields. First, let's mention the very language we use to name the elements at stake. The actual terms are confusing and they do not always express the meaning we are trying to convey. As an example, let's remember that in our Western languages we have inherited the Greek understanding of reality, and the word *spirit* expresses the opposite of the word *matter*. Consequently, "spiritual" describes that which is not "material" or, in terms of human behavior, someone who does not care about material things. A spiritual person would be one who does not take care of the needs of his body or places them in the background. Further, the Greeks differentiated practical life (*bios praktikós*) from contemplative life (*bios theoretikós*). The first corresponded to those who performed manual tasks—most of the people. The second corresponded to thinkers, philosophers, and artists, who studied the "spiritual sciences" and who were in those days a minority, free from the need to perform manual labor in order to sustain themselves. Thus, we inherit the assumption that thinking is an activity different from what is material and concrete, while physical tasks seem to tear us away from spirituality. On the contrary, in the biblical Hebrew—the language of the Old Testament—*spirit* comes from the term *ruah*, literally "wind," and by extension breath of life, living breath, breathing. There is a *ruah*-spirit when there is life. Its opposite is death, not matter. In biblical times the death of someone—or of an animal—was determined when the "wind" from his nose could not be perceived. In the New Testament, *pneuma* ("spirit") is opposed to *sarx* ("flesh"), that is, to that which is fragile, perishable. In the Bible, spiritual means alive, something that grows and remains, something that holds the power blown into a person by God and that only God can give. At the same time, the authors and biblical characters were, in most cases, people who performed concrete manual tasks and, in a few cases, those we may characterize as "thinkers." Even so, we should distinguish between such roles as they were practiced in Greece, and on the other side, in the Eastern cultures of the biblical world. In the latter, the "wise one" was recognized by his fear of God, that is, for how he linked his life and thoughts to God's plan, and not because of his mental shrewdness. Grasping and explaining this difference in meaning may help us avoid unpleasant arguments and misunderstandings—even bitter judgments between believers—that mar the life of the church and complicate the mission.

Faith and Evangelical Action

Another field that adds to the confusion is the mutual lack of understanding that has marked the relationship between the spiritual dimension of the Christian life and the impetus this spirituality gives the believer for his involvement in the building of a fairer society and where human relationships are characterized by love and solidarity instead of rivalry and exclusion. Some people have expressed this difficulty by introducing it as a dualism between prayer and Christian action that splits both aspects of the life of faith. Nevertheless, prayer as the culmination of spirituality, and action as the product of Christian solidarity, when separated, distort each other. But experience from past decades shows us that there have been Christians who, in their efforts to commit to social action, have experienced some suspicion of spirituality, at least the way it has traditionally been introduced. This happened because spirituality was understood as some kind of shelter where those believers not willing to commit themselves to the social field found the opportunity to nurture their faith away from society and its conflicts. From a certain perspective, this spirituality was not seen as an evangelical option linked to a specific way of living faith and a relationship with God, but as a conservative political option, more or less hidden behind a religious discourse.

From another point of view, we find those believers who watched with concern the political commitment of a group of brothers and sisters in Christ. They believed that their social commitment would end up weakening their spirituality. They observed that, to some extent, this made the person dedicate himself to material issues, and even resort to some kind of violent act or making concessions with the usual means for political struggle. This seemed to be the reason leading them to neglect their faith. The connection between faith and its demands, and social and political practice, was not always so evident. It was noted that political options split families, people, and the church. Old friends and brothers were distanced by an element *external* to the faith, one that originated outside the church's circle. What is more, the church as a community felt that the political issues threatened its fraternal and communal life, since its claims disrupted the harmony of congregational life. For such an understanding of life and faith, cultivating spirituality ensured some kind of connection to the transcendent, which did not allow being distracted by momentary tasks or becoming enthusiastic for fleeting human achievements and did not risk the integrity of the community, but strengthened it while preserving it from ideas considered strange to its identity and specific mission, as it is manifested in the gospels.

Criticism and Self-Criticism

Both stances, although most of the time assumed with sincerity by the church, are fundamentally wrong, and we need to criticize them so that later on we can commit ourselves to contribute positively to the construction of a spirituality coherent with the gospel. We should remember that spirituality is a way of living, not so much a way of thinking, and that this places us in a different position in regard to its questions and the search for its answers. The critic will also have to be an honest self-critic or else he or she will not be consistent.

The social commitment taken in the name of Christian faith that ignores what is transcendent in history and presumes the full realization of God's promises exclusively in human history should be considered a simplification of the biblical message. The novelty of God's message in the Bible is that the transcendent has entered human history, that God has become one of us (John 1:14). The biblical stories are full of examples where the character marvels when running into signs of the presence of God in simple places and somehow unexpected ways. Let's remember Elijah who, after he had experienced wind, an earthquake, and fire, encountered God in a gentle breeze (1 Kgs 19:11–12). The text does not lead us to say that God *was* the breeze; neither would we say that God was *like* the breeze. The story deals with God Himself, who communicates and who reveals Himself as the one behind the whole pilgrimage of the prophet who fled to save his life. Along the same lines, we find the story in Luke 9:37–43, where Jesus casts out a demon and, after this act of healing, according to the text, "all were astounded at the greatness of God." We should note that the people present were not astounded by the healing miracle or the sudden good health of the young man. That which moved and touched them was the discovery that God had acted before them and that they had witnessed a clear, divine intervention. In such passages, "spirituality" does not consist of the character's attitude toward his inner self but in being able to perceive the presence of God where others feel only a simple breeze, or a person who for some inexplicable reason has recovered his health through the actions of an unknown man, who came from Galilee and is surrounded by undesirable people.

These brief thoughts lead us to state that there is no room for a *passive* understanding of the being and doing of God, as a reduction of his actions to the mere flow of the natural laws that, being created by Him, constitute now His only way for action. God is not a necessary hypothesis so that the world makes sense, but rather a real presence that modifies the life of the believer and, through it, the history of human beings. In other words, and following the matter through to its end, we may be placing ourselves within deism, which accepts the existence of the divinity but does not believe in its personal intervention in the lives of people and in history. It is the already classic image of a little God who, having created the world and set things in motion, has gone to sleep eternally and remains indifferent to our personal and communal destiny.

This same thinking allows us to make some constructive comments on the attitude of those brothers and sisters who are looking for a more spiritual life, moving away from everyday life, or taking shelter in "God's things." It is true that the Gospels show Jesus leaving to pray alone, expressing the need for personal dialogue with God and setting apart some time so that this task is not disrupted by others. We believe that we have paid little attention to those moments in the life of Jesus that carry a specific significance in His own way of praying and that are a sign of the mature relationship between the believer and his Lord. Nevertheless, Jesus' attitude must be considered just as it is presented in the gospels, that is, as part of his ministry, when there were moments of doubt and weakness, which reveal His commitment with human beings, shared with other moments when the glory of God was evident in His actions and words. Thus, the relationship Jesus develops with His Father is nurtured by those moments when He leaves in order to be with God in the intimacy of prayer. When the gospels show Jesus in conflict with Himself because of the need to be obedient to the Father—the prayer at Gethsemane might be the most dramatic example—we are introduced to a Jesus who so identifies with humanity that we have no room to think that we will be nearer to Him if we distance ourselves from our neighbors and their problems. Jesus is with the people in solidarity, accompanying the suffering and highlighting the hypocrisy of the religious elites and rulers. This provoked the rejection of those who were *also* loved by Jesus and to whom His message was a call to salvation by showing them a different way to develop relationships between people and society. In this the strength of Jesus' spirituality is evident. Jesus, as an example for our own spirituality, saw in the flesh and bones of His fellow men the real image of God as stamped on them. Only a frivolous look would have ignored His real body and pain in order to propose a spirituality disassociated from real life. Consequently, when it comes to addressing issues of social justice, human rights, health care or educational development, these actions are not strange to faith and spirituality; on the contrary, they are ways to bear witness to God's interest in His creation and through which He listens to His children when they cry out in their suffering and marginalization.

6

The Spirituality of the Believer

Christian spirituality is the most adequate sphere in which to define the believer's relationship with Christ. Let's make clear what we are talking about so as not to mix it up with biblical spirituality. We should also ask ourselves about the relationship between the spirituality of the believer and the reality of the church where such spirituality is experienced.

Let's start by saying that as human beings, we have a spiritual dimension that constitutes our lives. As in other spheres of our lives, it can be channeled correctly or distorted to the absurd. It is important to understand that we are stepping onto a slippery slope, where not all spirituality is Christian (though this does not mean that it may be harmful for somebody or the group around him), and that at the same time, there are forms of spiritual practice that are not only not Christian but that distort an actual relationship with God. Let's see what we are referring to.

Spirituality is the openness of a person toward somebody or something different from himself through which he feels completed. Friendship is a spiritual relationship. Love as a couple is a spiritual relationship. We could offer other examples of relationships in which the relationship is established based on intangible values and which demand fidelity and commitment. Some cultural or national loyalties have a high spiritual component: they are not constituted by material, economic, or meager interests but by the individual's feeling and links to a certain identity, no matter what his own interests are. For a relationship of this type, sacrifices are made, freely giving up what we most want and even offering up one's life.

One of the most interesting spiritual relationships is the one we establish with art. The person who feels sensitized in front of a painting, a poem, or a melody, or who feels the deep impact of a novel in his life, has developed a specific—and spiritual—relationship with the other reality developed by the work of art. The artist has bestowed something to his work that acts through empathy with other individuals beyond the limits of time, geography, and even cultures. The artist puts his most private feelings down onto the canvas that will later on be contemplated—after several centuries—in a different cultural and social context the author could not possibly have imagined. But there is something in that painting that touches a private feeling in today's observer. This is a spiritual bond, and as such it cannot be explained, but it is real and leads one who experiences it to develop a more profound and intimate relationship with oneself and with other people. Spirituality opens inner doors leading to new places, sometimes profound and unknown, that go deep into the human experience.

What There Is Inside

This spirituality, present in every person, is that which takes the Christian faith and extends it toward outer circles. It is interesting to take into account that Christian faith is not built in opposition to the spiritual values already in the individual; on the contrary, it maximizes those values and gives them a distinct reference, not only in its origin but in its object as well. Christian spirituality differs from others in that it has its origin in Christ and its object in the neighbor, but it is built based on human experience and not on an unknown and immaterial place. It is wrong to believe that everything that naturally flows out from people, if it does not have a direct reference in Christian faith, has no value or—even worse—belongs to the world of sin. Friendship, love, and dignity exist far beyond an explicit reference to our faith, and conversion does not invalidate those values, but Christ's presence elevates them even more. From the perspective of faith, this experience shows that the Holy Spirit acts beyond the walls of the church and beyond our own perception of what should be its action in our lives and in the world.

It should be clear enough for us that we are referring to those spiritual experiences that contribute to elevating life, to dignifying and enriching it, and not to all those things that degrade and destroy it, which are abundant in our times (as they were in previous ages) and which can also be considered spiritual experiences. The feeling of emptiness and despair that has overwhelmed Western society in the last decades, combined with a lack of perspective and real hope, have produced a search for alternatives in order to fill in the gaps. It is difficult to determine if this diagnosis is justifiable, but it is true that there has been a boom in the search for meaning in life because many perceive that everyday reality has no clear direction. What happens is that when this search produces no healthy answers, it triggers harmful behaviors in individuals and society. In this sense, we may understand the use of narcotic drugs as mainly a spiritual problem that besets people who feel their lives are worth nothing, that it is the same to exist or not to exist, and that whatever their aspirations may be, in the end they will be nothing more than a number in a computer. At the same time, it is not strange that in these days other social phenomena have emerged that reveal despair and disappointment in life. From the cruel economic planning that impoverishes millions of people to the collective suicides agreed to via the Internet, we might find other examples that show that we are living in a society in the midst of deep spiritual turmoil. Beyond the fact that we reject instinctually the destruction of one's own life, when analyzing the reasons leading some people to choose such a path, we note that there is an almost total lack of expectation in terms of both the present and the future. The spiritual bond with life—something we cannot define but that we feel is there and pushes us to go on living—is broken. What is there in the lives of those individuals who escape from reality or who are looking for a premature death? What are their ideals, and what does society offer them in the way of assistance in developing those ideals? Did they have the opportunity to develop their potential so as to be able to choose something different for their lives? There might be individual answers to explain the psychological reasons in each case; the social phenomenon is not explained by individual conflicts or by the existence of criminals who become rich by poisoning people. These contemporary tragedies mark the lack of meaning in life and the spiritual vacuum we have fallen into as a culture and as a civilization.

Christian Spirituality

For the believer, spirituality cannot be disassociated from understanding the biblical message. In the Bible we find the raw material needed to build a relationship with God that we call spirituality. The problem is not in "being spiritual"—as we have already said, there is a natural trend toward this—but in what kind of spirituality gives meaning to our lives. Because this same human nature that looks for meaning in life and death through spiritual ways of developing relationships also offers a quick and successful alternative when creating substitutes to stand for real faith and real spirituality.

We should acknowledge that there are ambiguous values in spirituality. The same things that draw us close to God may draw us away; what helps us see more clearly can also obscure our understanding. At this point, a biblical passage comes to our aid. When perusing the pages of the Bible we find that spirituality is shown in being able to perceive God acting in human history. Let's look at an example from the Old Testament.

In Exod 3:8 we find a masterpiece of storytelling, but also a context that demands a deep spirituality to understand it in its whole dimension. It reads:

> ... and I have come down to deliver them from the Egyptians, and to bring them up out of that land to a good and broad land, a land flowing with milk and honey, to the country of the Canaanites, the Hittites, the Amorites, the Perizzites, the Hivites, and the Jebusites.

Two verbs are used ("to come down" and "to bring up") to describe God's action and the action of God's people. God comes down from His place in order to meet His people. The image of God being "up" is very old, and though we recognize it as a way of speaking—because God is everywhere and not only "up"—it is a symbolic expression of the distance between our situation (we are people walking on the surface of the earth) and God, who is beyond our limitations. So, it is said that God came down to His people, but also that God "brings them up" from where they were. The expression "bring up" in many cases is used to refer to going to Canaan, particularly to Judah and Jerusalem. Given that this region corresponded to the area of the high hills of Judea, and that Jerusalem will be situated on the top of one of them (Mount Zion), in order to arrive there from almost every corner it was necessary to go "up" the slopes. In our verse, the use of the verbs "to come down" and "to bring up" has a denser value. God takes the initiative in both cases, and when coming down and bringing up Israel, they meet in the middle. So God agrees to come down to the bottom, where His people are—to come nearer—and from this point we are taken by God to encounter Him. Note that it is not Israel who searches for God, but God who summons Israel to meet Him halfway. The encounter promoted by God takes place somewhere that is neither God's dwelling place (where only He can enter in order to avoid our appropriating Him) nor the land of slavery (where the Israelites were living and from which He wants to save them). The space for spirituality is a place created by God so that the believer encounters Him and walks by His side.

And for what is He calling us to this spiritual encounter with Him? What is He planning? God called the Israelites to offer them a life project that would change their slavery into freedom, their servitude into service to God and neighbor. The verse expresses such a project when it says He will lead them to a land different from the one they now inhabit. This land is described in three different and complementary ways: it is a good and large land, one where there is plenty of food, and one already inhabited by other people. It is necessary to try to imagine how the Israelites were surprised by this description of the promised land, because the land where they were living in Egypt at the time was very good and wide, produced a thousand times more food than Canaan, and was inhabited by only one nation. Some even believed that God was calling them to leave a land where, though they were poor, they could at least live without surprises—although they forgot the failed genocide at the hands of the Pharaoh, perhaps because, confronted with the challenge of being a free people, they felt a nostalgia for the "good old days"—in order to move to a dubious and already inhabited place, without knowing if they were going to be welcome. They could not see that the difference was not in the quality of the land or its width, but in the relationship they were going to develop with the land: while in Egypt they were producing for other people, in the land God was offering they would enjoy the fruits of their labor. The promise consisted mainly in that in such a place they would be able to work and grow as individuals and as a people, since the bond between them and the land was given by God, the Creator and Giver of all gifts. There they would acquire an identity and would be able to raise their children without fear, in a place where God had promised to be with them forever.

An attentive reader may notice that the verse mentions the people living in Canaan in those days, and so it is almost impossible to avoid asking, "What kind of gift is God giving if the land already belongs to other people?" This question will be answered throughout the biblical text, but we can see that this verse makes no reference to the conquest of land. It does not say that it is necessary to expel those residing in Canaan to make room for Israel. It's like saying that there, where six nations were living, Israel would become the seventh and share the territory ("there's always room for one more," the text seems to be saying). The theme of expulsion and war for conquest will come up in later passages, but at that moment God announces that at that place they will be able to peacefully coexist with other nations. The curious thing about the story of the arrival in Canaan is that, though it is about the conquest, the war and the expulsion of the Canaanites, the biblical stories are full of examples of how, in reality, the Israelites never expelled them but coexisted with them and shared the land.

Trying to grasp the meaning of this project of God for Israel was the most demanding spiritual task that men and women had to face at the time, since the faith they were asked to have did not arise from their human nature but from their willingness to move to that place created by God to meet Him and receive His instruction. Their ability to perceive the difference in God's history, voice, and action among us was tested.

Spirituality and the Church

Evangelical faith has a very strong component in personal devotion. Personal devotion is a value that should be preserved because relationship with God will always consist of a personal dialogue and will demand a personal decision from us. This personal dialogue refers to a larger community of men and women called by Christ to perform their mission on the earth. The stories from the gospels clearly show that Jesus called, one by one, each of His disciples to form a group of people that should act in an organized way. We have already seen that the image of being the "body of Christ," where each member performs an essential function that no other member can fulfill, is perfect to describe the church. Thus, the affirmative answer to God's call makes us part of His church, and it is there where we should first experience spirituality.

There are two elements that balance one another where the church is revealed as central to our spirituality. A tension exists between the two elements. On the one side there is spirituality; in its search to attain everything it is always in the process of growing into other areas of life. But on the other side it is necessary to have a parameter that accompanies such growth, conducting spirituality so that it remains an expression of Christian faith and does not revert to models that will finally impoverish it. Both elements can be described as follows.

Personal spirituality, when trying to expand, finds reality in exterior spaces where it is deepened. We discover that people around us are not mere partners on the road of life, but windows to something deeper and more significant. Our own privacy is a window to understanding and finding ourselves, to recognizing that we are more than what stretches between our hat and our shoes. In this private exploration there are no limits because it is a route to the human and a road that God has created in us.

The church is the frame for this movement of expansion. The church by its very essence reminds us that we are not the only ones called by God and that we are not alone in carrying out His mission. In addition, it reminds us that the spirituality needed to be part of the community called church presumes the acknowledgment of the neighbor—both those who believe and those who do not, together as a permanent reference to Christ, who is the source and end of all Christian spirituality. In the church, spirituality is nourished and corrected by comparison to the experience of other brothers and sisters who are part of the same search.

7

The Missionary Church

The last passages in the Gospels of Luke and Mark disclose the mission that the resurrected Christ imparts to his disciples. The Gospel of Luke extends this announcement into the book of Acts, while the Gospel of John includes it in several passages. After reading them, the reader has the feeling—and we may say the certainty—that there is still something to be done, that God's message goes on and there are still challenges to be met. Those "unfinished" issues are the ones the Lord leaves in the hands of the church. Therefore, the mission of the church is not an incidental task but one that is revealed as essential to its existence and its *raison d'être*. And so we ask, "Of what does this mission consist?"

When reading the Gospel of Mathew, we will come across three assigned tasks, which are presented in this order: make disciples, baptize them, and teach them to live according to the message of Jesus. But it is striking that, of the three, baptism in the name of the Father, the Son, and the Holy Spirit is the ritual by which the believer will be incorporated into the church and will begin to follow the path of faith. It is curious because baptizing is a different activity since it is something specific, while announcing the gospel and educating in the faith are actions that last over time and are never completely accomplished, at least until the end of time, which exceeds all of our calculations.

Thus, we discover that we face a natural string of events starting with the announcement of the gospel, followed by the incorporation into the church through baptism of those who affirmatively answer the message and continue with the task (beginning at that precise moment) of walking the path of faith, living life with a new perspective. In this sense, we may say that the mission arises from the same nature of the triune God and puts in motion the totality of the experience of the relationship between believers and their God. There are successive movements starting with God the Father sending His Son to bear witness to the redeeming will and commitment of God with humanity; then it continues with the Son, bearing witness and illustrating the Father's will through His own words and actions; and the Son sending the Holy Spirit to act in the world as support and company for those who believe in Him.

There is a last movement in addition to these three. It consists in the triune God sending the church to continue the mission God has already initiated. In the development of God's revelation, this stage becomes a new movement in which each member has been assigned a place and responsibility in the communication of the gospel. Consequently, the church is an entity created for such mission and not as an end in itself. God's mission goes beyond the church. As for its *raison d'etre,* the church cannot entrust others with what gives meaning to its existence: the church is called—above all—to be a missionary church.

The Mission's Three Dimensions

Being specific in regard to the mission of the church, we should highlight three aspects that express its diversity and richness. We are referring to witness (*martyría*), service (*diakonía*), and communion (*koinonía*). The three aspects are distinct, but together they constitute the church's mission. Let's consider each of them.

The witness of the church is a fundamental element of its mission. The Greek word *martyría* (which means "testimony") recalls those times in the church when bearing witness could (as it still may) lead to martyrdom and death. But its dimension is marked by the need for "saying" everything the believer knows about salvation in Christ. Testimony is telling other people of the origin of our behaviors and choices. It may be that, when putting into action the other dimensions of the mission (particularly when serving others, but on some occasions it might also happen with communion among believers), the Christian is drawn to act in secular environments and places where the faith of the participants is neither the reason for the gathering nor does it take up a specific place. Therefore, explaining the reasons why we choose a specific option is part of the mission we should put into action.

Bearing witness to our faith is also a task that takes us back to the core of the faith. The Christian faith is a faith proclaimed, announced, that is lived when sharing it. There are very few examples in the Bible of a faith lived in loneliness, disconnected from others. On the contrary, each character highlighted in the biblical stories is always introduced as related to other persons, whether for their blessing or as an example of what draws them apart from God. Jesus did not preach his message in solitude. It seems that the Scriptures were telling us that the biblical faith needs to be constructed with God and others.

The next dimension is service to others. The Greek word *diakonía* expresses this aspect that has to do with the bond between the church and the reality that surrounds it. Times change and each individual has his own challenges, but it is clear that the church cannot remain indifferent to what is going on around it. If we say that God is the Creator of the universe, we should assume that the whole creation is cared for by Him and that our task is to work on this creation to express God's will. This is the dimension that tries to show God's love for all of humanity, particularly for those suffering and bearing the consequences of injustices and cruelty. Christian *diakonía* has several aspects, but we should differentiate the *diakonía* exercised by the church through its direct action from the believer working beyond the limits of the Christian community. Both of them are part of the mission of the church and should be considered a task to which everybody is called. Those who serve others in the church, like those who serve through social organizations that are not linked directly to the church, must understand their work as a contribution to the church that is more mature in its mission.

The bonds between service and testimony are evident. Serving those in need or those who are waiting for a word of faith and encouragement is offering a testimony of the love of Christ to that person, who may or may not be a believer, or who may or may not understand the faith that motivates us. He or she receives our assistance—the visible act of love for others—but through us it is the love of God that is being expressed, the invisible act of God's love. If we are willing to be faithful to the unity of the church's mission, it is necessary that the visible act show the faith it is based on and refer to the invisible act implicit in it.

And here we must be clear. It is not just to proselytize or introduce our faith as the only force capable of carrying forward a project of solidarity and the transformation of society; this would be a mere act of evangelical clericalism—unfortunately, a more and more frequent problem—and would impoverish the church's testimony. And we cannot pretend that the believer is the only one who can love the "other" and be supportive. We would not only be denying the value of commitment of other people but we would be unaware that loving our neighbor is likewise demanded in other religious expressions (in Judaism, for instance, and in native religions) and is also an ethical value of philosophies and social choices, sometimes with no religious link. What we are trying to achieve is not to conceal the source of the strength of the church and to make evident that it is faith that gives meaning to our actions. There are two theological consequences to this statement.

The first warns us that the church, when serving others, might believe it has a right to receive a heavenly remuneration. We serve and love others as a way to show gratitude for the grace received and in the context of the peace of spirit received when knowing that Christ has already done what was needed to save us. Thus, the love the church expresses when working for the benefit of others is a love that does not belong or come out from its own entity, but is a reflection of God's love previously poured out into it.

The second is related to the collaboration with those who do not manifest a faith like ours and, in spite of this, they commit themselves to the service of others. This, instead of disturbing the Christian, should lead him to discover the action of the Holy Spirit beyond the walls of the church, and even of the Scriptures it has given us.

We celebrate with joy that men and women belonging to other confessions or secular thinking coincide with our ethical principles and that we gather together when working to make them true. But Christians must be conscious that theirs is an evangelical option, though other people embrace the same commitment from a different angle, faith or simply because they are moved by the sensitivity of the cause that unites them. This does not mean our option is truer or deeper, but it does mean that it has a double concern since it looks at the neighbor and looks at Christ. In other words, we see Christ in our neighbor.

The third dimension is *koinonía*. The communion (*koinonía*) of believers is a gift of God that we do not always acknowledge. It is the building of the Christian community as a place to share faith and life. It is the place for gathering and mutual understanding. The *koinonía* between believers should be like the relationship between God and His children. Just as God relates to us through love, in the same way we are called to relate to one another in the church. Nevertheless, this must be understood as part of the unity of the mission and not as an option among other possibilities. If there is no *koinonía* there is no church, as there is no church without testimony or service. This does not mean that in the church there will not be dissent, discussions, and even opposing points of view; if all these occur in the context of a healthy community relationship of love and understanding, the differences will be perceived as diversity and enrichment in the church and not as a competition to impose criteria. At the beginning of chapter 6 we pointed out that the church as a community is not perfect, and we reassert that statement now. Perfection is not a requirement for a Christian community; what is needed is to be ready to offer our best and to accept that we are not the only ones in the church.

The Church in Missionary Attitude

From the above exposition we understand that the mission of the church affects every aspect of its life. If we understand it in this way, we may say that the mission of the church is accomplished when the church is ready to take on a missionary attitude. Thus, from caring for creation to the quest to bring salvation to all, from promoting solidarity and justice for everybody to providing accessible and good translations of the Bible, from comforting the sick to helping those who have been beaten—all these actions are part of the mission of the church and they take place and are fulfilled in human history. Though there is a risk that the church could fall prey to at any moment. Embracing such a broad understanding of the church's mission, one that seems to include everything, is a risk, and we know there is a short distance between "everything is" and "nothing is." If we were to say that *everything* is mission, we would have to say that *every activity* is also mission. And without a doubt it is not. How can we overcome this situation?

The mission must not turn into some kind of universal, civilizing business that would end up replacing the specific task entrusted to the church. At this point, it seems right to go back to the fundamental passages of faith and look for orientation. When we read the narratives of the life of Jesus, it is evident that they testify that He came to bring *salvation*, and, beyond our own understanding of the concept, that was understood by His contemporaries as *good news*, or *gospel*.

The mission of the church is to announce this gospel and to invite others to adopt it as a governing principle of life. The mission of the church is—to put it simply—to evangelize. By our criteria, to evangelize is a highly contextual task that goes from the most simple—to pray for someone who is experiencing a particular situation, to teach in Sunday school—to more complex activities such as taking part in social movements that work for justice and equality among peoples and individuals. But what is unique about the *evangelizing* mission is that reference to faith is explicit and the invitation to come to Christ is something that does not need to be read between the lines because it is a clear and concise offer.

There are certain criteria that can orient us on how to achieve the perception of the church as having an *evangelizing mission*. These criteria are never pure or complete, and generally, we should look for some partial signs that will confirm that the criterion is being reached. At least one of them should be present in every activity of the church. We will mention five of them:

1. Church activities should, in one way or another, refer to the faith they are based on. What the church does should make evident that the church's task and meaning is to announce the good news of the gospel to everyone. Many times we may assume that a reference to faith is implicit in what the church is doing, but though in most cases it must be so, in others the testimony can be weakened if the intention is not explicit.

2. Through its activities, the church should contribute to the growth of its participants' faith. From growing in spirituality to deepening in the message of the Scriptures, what the church does should nurture a growing faith and an approach to Christ. In order to perform its mission, the search for a more mature faith must be a conscious act in the church's activities.

3. The church must contribute to fostering the life of the congregation. It should create links among its members and encourage the development of a community of people who, united, offer witness to Christ.

4. The church should encourage and support the participation of the believer in secular life and in social organizations that contribute to justice, culture, and social development. At the same time, it should train its members so that this participation also becomes a place for witnessing to the faith as it moves them.

5. Whatever the church does, it should invite us to faith in Christ. We are not always conscious that, when we assist someone in his or her need, or when we advise someone in trouble, if we do not accompany this action with an invitation to embrace faith, we are not offering the best of the church. If we do not communicate this faith that gives a foundation for the life and existence of the believer, the mission of church will be incomplete.

PART 2: Christ and Us

8

Who Do We Say He Is?

When posing a question about Christ's identity we are also asking about the identity of the church that proclaims Him and recognizes Him as Lord. When Jesus of Nazareth asks His disciples, "Who do the people say I am?" they answer with the names of three dead men: John the Baptist, Elijah, and Jeremiah. Then, Jesus continues with His question, but now directs the question to them: "Who do you say I am?" Peter's answer must have sounded very strange: "You are the Christ"—that is, the Messiah, the Anointed One of God (Matt 16:13–16). How do we answer the question? Our answer will reveal the kind of church we are, and for that reason, this old question of Jesus resonates in our day, and each generation must provide its response.

Christ and the Christs

Let's begin with a statement made by the Danish theologian Søren Kierkegaard: Christ is the eternal contemporary. Now, let us focus on the relationship between the eternity and the contemporaneity of Christ. The statement above concentrates the questions on the universality of Christ, that is, the ever-Christ, the Christ of our grandparents and our grandchildren and his specific ways of being made real—the ways in which He is contemporary to us, today's Christ, the one who goes out to meet us every day, who speaks our own language. Who do we say He is?

First, we should ask ourselves about Christ as presented in the biblical narratives. This is not the place to summarize the content of the gospels, but it is known that each of them reflects a specific view of Christ and is related to the context in which the text was produced—and also that those diverse views coincide in the essentials and give us a profile of that man from Galilee who reveals Himself as the Son of God through His preaching of the nearness of the kingdom of God and the fullness of time and announces this to everybody willing to listen. Thus, the gospels show us a person who does not stand still but goes along the path mingling with people (the first name given to Christians was "followers of the way"), preaching in towns and villages and calling people to have an encounter with God.

The gospels show Jesus speaking to the people, particularly to those marginalized and despised in those days. Jesus met with those considered impure, like the sick, the corrupt, the tax collectors, the unfaithful, the prostitutes, the sinners, the poor. They all were called to faith and commitment to the kingdom of God that—in his own words—"is at hand." Today we know that this phrase refers to Jesus himself, that the kingdom is at hand when He is close to us.

Further, the biblical narratives show Jesus challenging the powerful and extolling the weak and humble. He did not get along with the priests or the scholars of his days. Some of them were upset because He was open to changing the traditions, most of which had no basis in the Scriptures (our Old Testament) or corresponded to a mechanical and literal reading that did not respect the spirit of the law. The others were concerned by His questioning of the authorities and hierarchies, particularly because He challenged the honesty of the exercise of their power.

Finally, it is necessary to say that the life and message of God in Christ do not end in any of the gospels. These are given so that from faith we encounter the Christ proclaimed in the evangelical narratives.

Second, we may try to identify Christ through the experience and the celebration of His life that the church performs today (also, of course, of the Christ that was celebrated through the past centuries). Just as a pebble thrown into a pond generates wider and wider ripples, the image of Christ goes from the small circle of personal, private devotion to the larger places of meeting with others and society. It is the black Christ of the slaves, the poor Christ of the hungry, the secularized Christ of the postmodern inhabitants of our big cities. It is that Christ who is present when we give thanks for the joy of a party, and also that Christ with whom we share the bitter experiences of pain and loneliness.

These images of Christ are developed from the experience of that Christ who walked on the earth, lived and died as a limited human being, as limited as we are—and for this reason, when we recognize our limitations and fragilities, we get closer to Him. Because Christ was a Jew, he can be re-created by the indigenous or through our regional identities; because he was a genuine man, the experience of being a genuine woman can be deeply understood; because he was marginalized religiously, He can be understood by the faith of the church.

The contemporary Christs reveal that we can understand His persona and His message through His human shape. God became flesh so that those who do not understand a language different from their own have a limited, though blessed, human life and may have access to His full comprehension.

At this point, it is essential to ask if these "contextual Christs" are only mere ideological and cultural projections and not the "true" Christ. If every social sector, every historical background, and every personal experience "develops" its own Christ, are we turning Him into a God of our own likeness? In such a case, it would be a functional Christ for a specific political or cultural project, whether we like it or not. This is always a risk and a temptation for the church and for every Christian. When we act in such a way, not only do we act from the worst sort of fundamentalisms but we reduce Christ to our own pettiness.

It is then that we need to rethink our specific understanding of Christ, which does not mean that we are going to question or weaken our faith but, on the contrary, that we hope that from this experience our faith will be strengthened. Presenting a definite and total Christ, with no room for rereadings or possible discrepancies, does not favor the cause of the faith and the church. This would be, from our perspective, a Christ distorted through manipulation and, consequently, a weak and inconsistent one.

The fact that the powerful have used and still use religion in their favor in order to oppress and dominate (as, for example, during the conquest of America or the so-called holy wars) does not authorize us to do the same from the other side of the street. In fact, when we develop a Christ to our own liking we empty the contents of the true Christ who reconciles and heals. And our Christ will always be less revolutionary than the true and real one who is the consequence of contrasting our contextual experience with the written word that describes Him and delivers His message.

We are not claiming an idealistic way of thinking, by which a perfect and ideal Christ becomes real through "imperfect" contextual ways. What we are asking for is to have the strength of character to recognize our own limitations and to be ready to always confront the understanding we have of Christ with the one delivered by the Scriptures. This attitude should be a central principle of faith, since it will allow us not to manipulate the Son of God by giving Him the shape and characteristics that resemble our own and so distorting Him that we are prevented from perceiving the true Christ presented in the Scriptures.

Who Do We Say He Is?

If we address this question to the first witnesses of Jesus' life, we will come across contradictory answers: to the Romans he was a political leader who considered himself a king; to the Pharisees he was an exaggerated idealist and a useless lawbreaker; to women he was a light that was lit and then extinguished; to revolutionary Jewish zealots he was weak and conservative; to the poor he was a prophet and a frustrated liberator who generated expectations that were not accomplished; and finally, to the thousands who saw Him passing through their towns and their fields, he was an enlightened man who ended up sentenced and killed. Let's pose two theological questions that will help us deal with this matter.

How to Talk about Christ Today?

We bear witness to Christ within the community that is the church. In the church we cultivate the Christ of faith, whom we invoke in our prayers and celebrate at the table. He is the Christ who gathers around Him a community of men and women, children and elders, the poor and the fortunate, the erudite and the uneducated. The diversity within the church is a testimony to a world more and more divided by numerous ways of classifying people. But when the church gathers, it has a purpose, and we should ask ourselves about the meaning of such a purpose.

It seems that the conflict between the traditional and the progressive church is not valid since both models express partly the goal of the church. While in one model the goal gives privilege to life within the church, to preserve the doctrine of faith and the development of a spirituality that is intimate and communitarian, the other tries to give social relevance to the church's mission, involving itself in political and social conflicts and exercising a prophetic voice outside the ecclesial circle.

From Latin America came the first warnings concerning the fact that, whereas the first model sought orthodoxy, the second gave importance to orthopraxis. Thus, the right doctrine ("ortho*doxy*") is opposed to the right action ("ortho*praxy*"). This categorization was useful when the exercise of the believer's social commitment was considered to be outside of proper doctrine. While on the one side came the charge of breaking Christian doctrine (or even perverting it), on the other it was said that the social praxis formed a new doctrine that was more similar to the processes of justice and liberation. This new doctrine invited a new way of spirituality "in action" and a new way of being church, one more committed to justice and the poor. No doubt, new theological spaces were discovered and barriers of ideological and social prejudices were broken down; however, an evaluation conducted at a certain distance shows that both models need and complement each other.

Today we know that the preservation and evolution of the doctrines of the faith are central elements of the action of the church. There is neither social nor political praxis if there is not a doctrine to support it, even when that doctrine should be reviewed and reformulated. On the other hand, the doctrine of the church should not be instrumental to an ideology, but should become a tool by which to address the challenges of the time and contribute to overcoming conflicts, promoting justice and truth. The church cannot cease asking itself what is going on in the society in which it lives, and it is called to bear witness in that place where it was planted, because a closed-door church has no future; neither does it have a present because, from the moment its doors are closed to the world, they are also closed to Christ. This way, as Christ moves us to go out into the world, the same Christ invites us to reflection, to prayer, and he will help us die when it is our time.

The Christ of the Church and the Christ of the Streets

Still, we may ask about the link between the Christ celebrated in the community of the church and that same Christ acting beyond its walls, enacting in history His salvation plan. Some years ago, it seemed easier to speak of "the God of history" or of Christ "Lord of history." There was some confidence that the natural forces of history would lead us to a better world, that going in such a direction was inevitable. Of course there was an awareness of all the trouble and suffering, but they were understood as the way in the desert that will lead to the generous and wide promised land. Cruelty and pain were clearly perceived, and their eradication was planned in the context of a relentless historical evolutionism (of a Marxist origin, but also liberal developmentalism) that offered ideological support to the fact that "ultimately" history would be benign to human beings. In such a way it was stated—without major problems—that God was behind every new stage of humanity in the way to the kingdom.

The author of these pages believes that today we are less enthusiastic with this kind of thinking, but we find it difficult to explain the reason why, if the Lord is the Lord of history, human history is so cruel and seems not to be moving toward a better situation. Why is there so much suffering, which seems to have no point or possibility of being redeemed?

This is not an easy question to answer within the framework of the society in which we live. Be it the hyperdeveloped society or the one of sharp contrasts in Latin America or in other parts of the world's most vulnerable regions, we are asked how Christ is present in the world where we say he is. We need to explain how the Christ we celebrate in communion is manifested in human history.

We believe that it is possible to offer an answer if we try to avoid the other, more common and escapist one. We should avoid giving an image of a disembodied Christ, perfect in His solitude and removed from all forms of contact with humanity. This should be avoided not only because it is an artificial Christ, unbiblical and false, but also because such a Christ walks against the people; it is a way to dominate Christ and through Him dominate people.

In our opinion, in a society torn apart by injustice and marginality, Christ is present when we feel pain while looking into the faces of those in pain. Christ is in the indignation we feel in the face of contempt toward the poor and forgotten of the world. Christ is in the family crying over the death of a loved one, in the watching over the hospital bed where the sick is dying, in the determination of the body of the disabled. Christ is in the battered woman trying to rebuild her life and in the innocent victims of an absurd war. He is in the silent weeping of dispossessed indigenous people, and in the cells where the condemned await the final fire. Christ is waiting for us on the corner with the unemployed, in the dark room where soul and life are wasted; but the face of Christ is not an icon to be contemplated.

Where He appears, He calls us, just as when He said "follow me" to those who would become His disciples. In spite of our imperfections, Christ also becomes human in those who fight for justice, in the peacemaker who risks his life, in the honest judge, in the generosity of those who share what they own, in those who denounce corruption. Christ is in those who neither bend before the temptation of money nor rest until the light shines and shows the real faces of the ever eternal and ever contemporary Christ.

9

Remembering Our Baptism (Who Am I?)

Baptism is the sacrament through which people are incorporated into the church. All churches agree on this statement, although the form and the ritual can vary significantly in each case. In some traditions, baptism must be done by complete immersion—and there is no other option—while others agree on pouring water over the baptized. Some denominations demand the baptism of adults—that is, persons who can offer a testimony of their faith—while others accept, and privilege, the baptism of children, based on the faith of their parents and godparents. While many churches believe that baptism cannot be repeated and reject the practice of "rebaptism," others understand that to baptize again is natural if the first baptism is considered not to be the true expression of the believer's faith, or if a change in his or her life makes the person feel that the previous baptism is not valid.

The controversies over these options were and are intense and no doubt are valid since they express deep convictions about the meaning of baptism. But to a certain extent they have led to concealing the central issue: through baptism we acquire an identity before God. In baptism we receive the name by which God will know us and by which our brothers and sisters in Christ will recognize us in church. The "Christian name" is the one we are given when being baptized and that, with the coming years, will be completely identified with us. This is a consequence of the convergence of two opposing realities: when being baptized we are totally alone before God; when being baptized we are totally accompanied by the church before God.

What Is Your Name?

In the traditions that baptize children, the minister usually starts the liturgy by calling the parents and godparents to the front to introduce the child to be baptized. A girl or a boy has been born and they wish to incorporate him or her into God's people through a public event. They have faith and wish that this new member of their family might also grow in such faith and be received within the community of the church as a member. It is not easy to imagine the fragility and solitude of a little baby in that moment. His or her limitations and the fact that he or she is so dependent are evident; his or her need for support, food, and care will perhaps never be greater. And in this state the baby is in front of God. Will the child doubt as Thomas did? Will he cry out like Job? Will she try to escape like Jonah? Will he deny Jesus three times like Peter did? The child is completely alone and defenseless: a baby can only live by the grace he or she receives. And this extreme situation of the child reflects that of the adults in the church in that, though we may believe we are self-sufficient, we should acknowledge that just like the little one we live by God's grace and that in spite of our sins and faults, the Lord decided to commit totally to our human condition.

In this context, the child will be given a name. It is interesting to observe that in some liturgies the rhetorical question, "What name do you give this child?" is included. The answer is one of those little things that may become immense. The person introducing the child says aloud the name the baby will carry as a sign and by which he will be recognized by his peers in the future. This combination of a particular name and a specific person will bring about a unique entity and will constitute the child's sign for the rest of his or her life. The child, and only the child, will be identified with that name. God will call him or her by that name.

The symbol of the name should not be lost in those churches where baptism is only for adults. We may deceive ourselves and think that the name already belonged to this baptized person since childhood and that, in this case, the name has little to do with his baptism. Yet, if we consider that through baptism we enter into a new life and a new relationship with God, we cannot deny that in that moment we are symbolically introduced to God, and from then on the baptized will know that God calls and identifies him by the Christian name, the same used by those who surround him and love him. Until that moment we believed that God did not know of our existence, that He did not care, and now, in baptism, we have discovered that God has known us forever by that name and that He calls us by it; we were ignorant and thought that He did not care for us, and now we know it was not so. God knew our name before our baptism. The difference is that we now know that He knew us from the beginning and we understand that that familiarity with our name is also present in the relationship God has established with us in our lives.

In those churches where the baptism of children is accepted, we can ask ourselves about the faith of the one being baptized: if the child cannot decide for himself, how can he be baptized? We know that, in the beginning, baptism was a rite for adults and that, during the first centuries after Christ's death, the Christian church started baptizing babies. This step had to do with the need to differentiate the Christian community from the rest of the Roman population, who worshiped the classic pantheon. For this reason, each family would baptize their newly born child to assure that the child would belong to the Christian community, and also as a witness before a society in which Christians were a minority.

To consider that the baptism of children was a tradition built on a secondary interest (i.e., to ensure that when adults they would not become pagans) would be a mistake, since behind a child's baptism was the endeavor to place a new person in the context of the faith of the community where he or she was baptized. Through this visible rite was expressed the faith of the child's parents and godparents that God received the child in the church and the congregation assumed the responsibility to educate and guide the child in the way of faith. The change consisted in this: to the baptism of adult believers—based on the faith of the baptized—was added the baptism of the newborn, based on the faith of the receiving community and that of the parents, who would lead the child to maturity as a believer. In the case of the baptism of children, it is assumed that the rite is not sustained in the rational understanding of the sacrament, in the sense that the baptized should *understand* the baptism, but in the faith of the church and parents who entrust the child to God. This way, the person to be baptized is considered part of a larger community and does not exist in isolation.

Though baptism is a moment when we are completely alone with God, it is also when we are very much accompanied. Baptism is celebrated as part of the regular worship service of the church and not in isolation. Thus, the presence of the congregation is a main element in baptism. The congregation is not just an audience, since it plays a role that cannot be delegated. As a small portion of the whole—God's people—it represents the totality (catholicity) of the church around the world, and its prayer for the baptized is the prayer of all the church in all times. When a person is baptized he does not join a fragment of God's people, but he is received by the universal church of Christ, whatever the denomination of the baptizing church.

Water and Words

In baptism, water holds a symbolic value that sometimes escapes us. Judaism in the time of Jesus practiced ritual baths to purify the body and make the person suitable for God. When Jesus is baptized in the Jordan River, he takes part in a ritual to which many persons resorted in order to reach salvation and forgiveness of their sins. Since the river's water ran with some strength, it was natural to think that when running along the body it would sweep away everything evil in order to clean us and restore us before God.

Also, being submerged places the person in a situation of death, a limit where life is not possible, and this allows us to express the conviction that in baptism there is a passing from death to life, and when we emerge from the water in victory and renew the air in the lungs, there is the feeling of being born to a new life. Death and resurrection are present in baptism. The symbol of water, which originally was that of washing away everything that should be removed from the sinner and cleansing him, became also the symbol of the access to a new life to which God invites the believer. This flowing water was so important that, in the many cases where there was not a river close by, when the ritual bath was performed in public or private pools, it was essential that water from a river or creek be poured into the pool in order to give the still water the condition of "living" water. A small portion of "living" water would allow the still water to have the symbolism of washing away and purifying.

Together with the water are the words that are said in the act of baptism: "I baptize you in the name of the Father, the Son and the Holy Spirit." The Trinitarian formula and the water are the elements that characterize the Christian baptism and are considered irreplaceable for the correct celebration of the sacrament, but these are not the only words involved. There is also a statement of faith that should be declared by the baptized—if an adult—or the godparents in the case of a child. These words are not accessories because they imply the succession of faith passed from one generation of believers to another and the will that this faith that is declared by the elders be the same that illuminates the days of the person who is being incorporated into the family of the church.

Magic or Faith?

Sacraments presume a dimension of mystery. Not everything can be rationally understood, nor should it be in order for us to enjoy God's creation. In fact, there are many things that move us and make us feel intensely that we cannot explain. Nevertheless, baptism has been surrounded throughout the centuries with a certain halo of mystery that can be confused with what we commonly call magic. What happens if by mistake the words of baptism are not said exactly as written? What happens if the person officiating is not authorized? These questions lead us to the core of the matter of whether the rite acts by itself in the sense that it secures the efficacy of what is announced or whether, like every act carried out by human beings, it shares our ambiguities and limitations.

The doctrinal statement broadly accepted by all Christians is that baptism (and all the sacraments) is an outward and visible sign of an inward and spiritual grace. The issue is whether the sign—which as such always points to something other than itself—is mechanically related to its meaning or if there is a distance between the sign and its meaning. In other words, whether water and the Trinitarian formula *confer* God's grace by themselves or whether they *manifest* what God has already done in the person who is being baptized. The Catholic and Orthodox position is that the rite bestows the grace and that a mistake in the formula invalidates it. This position leads to the statement that if somebody celebrates the rite with water and uses the correct words of the Trinitarian formula, the baptism is valid even if the celebrant was not authorized or if the person who receives it is not a Christian believer. This understanding of the sacrament poses a number of difficulties, but we believe the main difficulty is the idea that the celebrant of the sacrament holds power over the Holy Spirit to allow—or not—the pouring out of grace on the baptized person.

When we confuse in a single entity the rite (the visible sign) with the efficient action of God (the invisible grace), the words of the celebrant and his gestures are those that open or close the doors for the *act of God* to be performed. For an evangelical theology, it is necessary to critique and to warn of the risk of conditioning the freedom of the Spirit and giving it away with no restrictions to the pastoral and ecclesial administration. We should be very clear that the presence of God and His grace do not depend on our words or gestures but on God's free decision to come to us.

We should also warn of the common mistake in the evangelical practice of considering the sacrament of baptism a simple representation. If there is nothing in this act but words the wind blows away and water that soon evaporates because the true baptism is performed by the Holy Spirit and not by us, we come close to minimizing an act that our Lord has instructed us to seriously administer for the salvation of the world. Baptism is not mere mimicry but a sign and signal pointing to the death and resurrection of Christ—and to the promise of our own death and resurrection—who acted once and for always in favor of us all. That action of God is recognized by faith and expressed through baptism to the people who witness it. It is necessary to highlight that from the evangelical point of view, the presence and action of the Holy Spirit in the act of baptism is real and effective, and the proof of this should not be the perfect declaration of a formula—no matter how important it is—since the miracle of faith is present in all the people who share in the moment. The sacrament is valid if it is celebrated in the context of a community of true believers who are expressing their will to transmit their faith in Christ, who has saved them.

Baptism and Rebaptism

We would like to highlight two issues that come from these ideas. The first one is that it is not true that those who die and have not been baptized fall outside of the grace of God or will not gain access to the benefits of God's love. Some, when a little baby's life is in danger, turn to a rushed baptism in order to avoid such tragedy. In this sense, it is necessary to remind them that the grace and blessing of God on the child does not depend on a rite or on our own timing, because God has offered enough proof that His kindness and generosity exceed human limitations.

In these cases, no doubt baptism is valid as far as it shows the parents' faith and expresses their will that the Lord who gave life to the newborn may receive him back as His son or daughter. It can also be understood as an expression of gratitude by the parents for that little life that could not develop as expected, but has played a role in God's plan for everybody around him, even for themselves, but its absence does not exclude him in any way from the love of God or His infinite grace.

The second issue is related to the practice of rebaptism. In general, some churches consider it necessary to rebaptize people who have had a new encounter with God and explain such a theological understanding as invalidating the first baptism. This invalidation normally rests on the lack of a "personal experience" when baptism was celebrated originally—for having been baptized as a child—or because it was celebrated within a denomination in which there is not a shared comprehension of faith or Christian practice. To us, it is evident that the intention of rebaptism is noble and honest, and can also be understood as an impartial critique of the Constantinian model of the medieval church, which joined secular citizenship to belonging to a church. Today, that model persists, though not as much, in those countries where simply being born there implies belonging to a specific church and where Christian faith has been attached to a specific culture, and is sometimes is confused with purely social and passing ways. But even if we recognize the value of this critique of faith as culture—a critique we share and believe should be preserved and encouraged—we think that the practice of rebaptism suffers from the same limitations we have pointed out in the Catholic and Orthodox understanding.

It is thought that because something in the rite did not take the correct form, the baptism was not valid and, consequently, the person must be baptized again. Unlike those churches, for the traditions that do rebaptize, what went wrong is not related to the adequate use of water or the words in the baptismal formula, but with the supposedly imperfect faith of the baptized person or the attendants or the spiritual, doctrinal context of the officiating church. We are convinced that it is necessary to discontinue this attitude of some branches of our evangelical tradition.

If we carefully observe a baptism in almost every church, we will observe that when a minister from a Christian denomination celebrates a baptism, he or she does not do it in reference to the ecclesial authorities or by invoking the power of their specific doctrine. The sacrament of baptism is performed in all the churches within the frame of the Trinitarian doctrine and uses the symbol of water that washes and takes away everything that separates us from God. When celebrated this way, a baptism should not be rejected even when the doctrinal framework does not convince us. Not to acknowledge that this baptism is valid implies ignoring the freedom of the Holy Spirit that blesses and bestows its grace beyond the formula and gestures any denomination performs and the specific understanding of the doctrine each tradition has regarding what is truly happening in this act.

The second argument regarding the impossibility of the person being baptized to express faith is also serious and should be taken into account. The personal experience of recognizing Christ as our own savior and the savior of the world cannot be denied as a main ingredient of each believer's faith, but recognizing that dimension cannot allow us to disregard all the other faith experiences that are also personal and have been present in baptism and that are an essential piece of the sacrament. When the celebrant, the godparents, and the congregation have prayed, sung, and celebrated the glory of God, in that baptism they were not doing something without meaning or invoking an unknown God; on the contrary, they were asking for the guidance of God in the life of that child; and if the new adult experience of the believer is deep and has a spirit of renewal, it should be understood as an answer to the wishes and prayers expressed a long time ago by those brothers and sisters for that little child. When facing a new and renewing faith experience, instead of a new baptism what should be done is something richer and more challenging for the believer's faith: give thanks to God for the faith of those who took him to church and who poured out on him the blessing of the water. The testimony of those brothers and sisters—many of them perhaps unknown or forgotten—must be understood as the link with Christ's church yesterday and always that today is manifested in this new experience in the way of faith. The new experience of a renewed encounter with God is a continuation and consequence of that baptism, and not its denial.

10

The Lord's Table (Who Are We?)

The sacrament of the Lord's Table is the supreme act of communion. In this moment God communicates His strength and presence to the person receiving it and offers the certainty of His company in all circumstances. God invites the believer to partake of the bread and wine and, through this, to reaffirm his or her faith in Christ, which will always stay with the believer. There is also an eschatological dimension at the table, signified in the fact that the Lord feeds us in an essential way. In the past and present world, where hunger is a scourge for millions of God's children, the Lord has chosen to reveal Himself before us in the context of food, the act of sharing the bread placed on the table, this bread the world denies with the utmost cruelty. And this happens in a particular context: a table shared with others and an invitation that is repeated.

The Wide Table

Unlike baptism, in which we are alone before God and we are identified by a specific name that will be used to differentiate us from the rest of the people, in the sacrament of communion we stand together with the rest of our brothers and sisters in the church on an equal footing. Just as when we receive a personal invitation to a party we know that we will meet other people and share in the festivities with them, so we should understand God's invitation to His supper: we are personally called by our own names, but the party is not exclusively for us; we will gather with other people. This is why the Lord's Supper is a rite in which the believers are gathered—called by Christ—to participate in the major act of communion with Him and His church.

Two dimensions are present in communion that nurture each other and that cannot be excluded without invalidating the gesture. On the one hand, it is the table that joins us to Christ and His gospel. In this dimension the table offers the confirmation that, no matter what may happen, the Lord stays with us. This central statement of faith is made in the context of recalling the bitter night of the Last Supper, when Jesus lived the most tragic events in his life: the imminence of suffering, the announcement of his death, and—worst of all—the betrayal of a friend. The Lord's Supper is mainly the remembrance of the crucifixion, in which one of the main elements is the betrayal by one of the disciples and, in contrast, the affirmation that Jesus will never betray us, no matter the circumstances. If Judas acted in representation of many who yesterday and today betray and deny Jesus, Jesus, on the other hand, as the Son of God, totally commits Himself in favor of our lives, even the life of the one who gave Him over to his murderers. Thus, the Lord's Table is that place where we can clearly perceive the distance between our sins and His holiness, our deceptions and His transparency, our pettiness and His immense and freely given love.

The invitation to partake at the table is not only a mirror in which we face our pettiness and discover our faults. The table is essentially that place where we receive the grace to know that the Lord forgives us and receives us again as His friends. In that moment we can feel the strength of the good news of salvation resounding and that God remembers us and has a plan for every life. We also discover that, no matter how poor our conduct has been and how far we have fallen and have become separated from God, He will come to the darkest corner and will tell us that our sins are forgiven and that He wants us to be whole, working for His kingdom and being part of His team in mission. The Lord's Table is wide because there is room for all who accept the invitation. It is interesting to note that in the gospel narratives Jesus is shown sharing his table with the disciples, who are quite confused. They neither understand His words nor believe that they might betray Him, but then they argue about who the betrayer will be and who will succeed Jesus. So if we are looking for holiness, we are not going to find it on that day in the life of that group. On the contrary, this episode should make us think about how similar to us the disciples were in that moment.

There is a second dimension to the Lord's Supper, and it has to do with the unity that creates and calls the brothers and sisters. The table is the celebration of the community that, gathered around the elements, feels united to each other and by extension to the whole of Christ's church, at all times and in every place. The word *communion* means "to be connected" and in the supper refers to communion with God and at the same time with the community of faith, in such a way that both dimensions cannot be separated. Thus, the supper is the celebration in which the church is shown its greatest degreee of splendor and commitment. But it would be a mistake to consider that such union with God and the church is a consequence of our attitude when approaching the table. On the contrary, it is Christ Himself who works for unity among believers, and this is not based on our weaknesses but is because of His strength. His word develops in us. At the table unity is created from dissimilarity because there we are all respected in our individuality, and simultaneously we are joined with those who, because of our human nature, we would separate ourselves from because of our differences. So, coming close to share in the Lord's Supper leads us to the unity of the church in the small circle of those gathered, and also links all those who in different languages, cultures, times, and doctrinal approaches accept and have accepted throughout the centuries God's invitation. But it is necessary to point out that the unity the table is calling us to participate in goes beyond the limits of the universal church and becomes a glimpse of the gathering of the whole creation in the person of Christ for the redemption of the world. In that moment, not only is the past evoked but also the full gathering of the people with the Lord, the final meal when there will be no more thirsty or hungry people and when we will meet face to face with the last reality. Being received by God at His table opens our blind eyes to His action in our life, in the lives of others, and in the world, so that once we have tasted that food, we will not be able to ignore His love and kindness.

It is understandable that in the face of such revelation the answer of the believer is gratitude. The word *Eucharist*—the Greek word used to describe communion in the gospels—means "to give thanks." We thank God for the sacrifice of Christ on the cross that brought us salvation, which He offers to us freely. In the same way we have done nothing to deserve it, nothing can defeat the strength of the love poured forth that day in the death on the cross—a pain and a death of such physical and spiritual magnitude that it will not be necessary to endure them again.

Christ Is Present—but How?

The different Christian traditions do not agree on the significance of the sacrament of the Lord's Supper. In the Catholic understanding, in the act of the Eucharist the mystery of transubstantiation operates in a way in which the bread and wine are transformed into the actual body and blood of Christ. Obviously, this is a dogmatic statement and not a physical reality—since the flavor and texture correspond to bread and wine—but what is interesting about this understanding is the question it is trying to answer: is Christ truly in those elements? Or, in other words, how is Christ present among the community sharing the table He has prepared? While the questions are essential and deserve our utmost attention, the doctrine of transubstantiation seems not to do justice to the entire event of the sacrament.

Let's look at it from this point of view. One issue has to do with the understanding of Jesus' words "Do this in remembrance of me." When we remember something, do we actualize it or do we evoke it as a memory? A certain tradition understood that, if the Eucharist was *only* to remember past events, its value would diminish to such a point that it would not be possible to speak of the actual presence of Christ in the sacrament and, if there is no actual presence, the rite loses its value. And so developed the concept that every time the sacrament of the Lord's Supper is celebrated we actualize the original sacrifice and Christ is once again given and murdered for our sins. In this way, every time the bread is broken and the cup is drunk, the body of Christ suffers again and His blood is shed once more, and the real presence of the Lord is sealed in this act in the community of the church. There are two elements that this doctrine is not considering.

First, to insist in the repetition of the sacrifice minimizes the actual sacrifice of Christ endured in a place—the city of Jerusalem—and at a specific time—around 33 AD. That suffering and death were not physically different from others—for example, the suffering and death of the two criminals to his right and left at Golgotha. What made Christ's death different was the saving dimension and the cosmic extension that no other death had. At that moment, the forces of history were concentrated in that body that was dying on behalf of others and that was carrying in His death the sins of other people. The action of God in Christ was complete and nothing was left. Had this not been so He would have claimed it. Living the sacrifice once again is to consider that the actual and historic sacrifice—not a sacrifice in bread and wine transubstantiated, but in flesh and blood for its own nature—was not enough for our salvation.

Second, there is a Trinitarian dimension that seems not to be properly represented in the insistence on repeating the sacrifice at every Eucharist. The experience and testimony of the church through the centuries is that the death and resurrection of the Son is followed by the saving presence of the Holy Spirit. The church is alive thanks to the presence of the Spirit that *continues* acting in life and history, beyond the cross, and provoking new revelations and posing new challenges to the church. Within the Trinitarian economy, the action of the Spirit is always an opening to what is new in history subsequent to Christ's sacrifice on the cross, but that is not performed against what happened that day "in the city of Jerusalem, around the year 33 AD"—as if it were necessary for the Holy Spirit to do "something else" in order to complete that sacrifice—but that its saving action is made as a constant reference to that event recognized as central and complete and as the basis of its action. The completeness of the death and resurrection of Christ are evoked every time the Spirit works as a memory of the total sacrifice, and it is what makes it unnecessary to nail Jesus to the cross again or to repeat His resurrection.

There is also some trouble with the evangelical understanding of the Lord's Table. On some occasions it has been said that the bread and wine symbolically express the presence of Christ and that the Lord's Supper is a remembrance of the Lord's sacrifice, but as an event separated from its physical and spiritual reality. To be clear, the Lord is not in that bread and wine; they are only elements by which to remember Him, just as He said in the Last Supper with His disciples. In this attitude there is a lack of understanding of the nature of the sacrament that leads us to fail to grasp part of the transcendent and even eschatological dimension of what happens in the Eucharist. In our opinion, it is important to understand that Christ is a real presence in that bread and wine we are sharing in the context of the Christian community. It is for the eyes of faith to see what is invisible and, no doubt, it is not for those who with reasoning or mere intellectual speculation pretend to explain the wholeness of the human experience. If it is natural that we recognize the presence of God in human acts of love and solidarity, in the circle of prayer where we share joys and sorrows, in the stunning beauty of creation, in the harmony of the heavenly bodies or in the face of the tired and hungry, why not recognize Him in bread and wine when we are asking his blessing on them and when we have said "this is my body" and "this is my blood"? When Christ Himself said these words in the Last Supper, obviously he was referring to His own body present at that moment in front of His disciples and not to the bread and wine as such. These elements became privileged referents of his life, chosen by Him. Consequently, Christ was in those elements of the supper in a very real and true way, as He is in all the other places where we recognize the work of His hands and His presence. What should keep us from being reluctant to discover the actual presence of Christ at the table is to remember that He was the one who chose those elements—and not others—so that we can explicitly discover Him. He is in many places, we might say in every place, but He stipulated specifically bread and wine from the supper to signify him.

Bread and Wine

We should not leave aside a meditation on the election of Jesus. There were other elements, much more immaculate than bread and wine, to evoke Him. Clouds, mountains, skies are free of any human intervention and they are pure works of God. The many stars in the skies and the lilies of the field were occasion for observation and example in the Scriptures and might be more prestigious candidates than the ones chosen by Jesus. The solidity of a rock and the mysterious depths of the sea might also have been elected, but the Lord chose bread and wine. What is in these elements that they occupied such a position in the communication of the gospel? We believe that meditating on this issue will help us understand the deep meaning of the sacrament and who this God is who invites us to share his table.

Both bread and wine are the result of human work. They require a sower and a miller, and hands that will knead the dough and tend the oven. The same can be said about the wine: the labor of the winegrower and the industriousness of the winery must combine so that the grape juice turns into a good wine, the work of a craftsman. In the bread and the wine are the hands of women and men; there are many days of labor and the joy of a good harvest. They are anonymous hands: the hands of believers and unbelievers, of those deep in love and those being unfaithful; there are honest hands and tricky hands. They might be the dreaming hands of those waiting for change or the hands of a desperate man without hope—the hand of one who has lost the capacity to imagine or a generous hand. The hands that made the bread and the wine at the Lord's Table are not holy hands, nor the best; they may be the most expert or clumsy, the most beautiful or the most deformed by life and the passing of time. Jesus wanted it to be this way. Because the bread and the wine at the table are almost another form of incarnation, there we can discern Jesus in the middle of our history, even in the deepest and darkest places. These elements represent everything we are and help us see how, by His grace, He transforms the fraying fabric of human existence into the bread of blessing and the wine of abundant life.

If at the table we become Christ's church, it is also because to make the bread it was necessary that a multitude of grains of wheat cease to be and cede their strength and combine with the water and the yeast. The same happened to the grapes; they turned into juice and then into wine. These are no longer grains of wheat or grapes, but bread and wine. Thus, men and women, by the grace of God and His transforming power, become Christ's church. They are no longer the same because they have become a new reality that transforms them into a sign of the salvation to which the Lord invites us all.

11

Proclaiming the Word: The Third Sacrament?

The meaning of the word *sacrament* is "mystery," and *sacrament* is applied to specific rites in which the church testifies that the grace of God is given to the people. It is assumed that there is something in the acts of God that we cannot completely understand, but that the eyes of faith can clearly perceive. In such a context, a sacrament is not a mystery in the sense that it is something that is incomprehensible but because of the fact that its full meaning goes beyond our faculties and extends in time and space beyond what we can assimilate. For example, we understand God's love, but the extension of His love goes far beyond the limits of our knowledge. We know and understand the Lord's sacrifice, but His salvific implications exceed our human capacity and our imagination.

There are seven sacraments in the Catholic tradition; in the Orthodox tradition there is no specific number but rather an open list of sacraments. In the evangelical tradition there are two: baptism and the Lord's Supper. Also, all traditions accept that there are other acts or practices that have a sacramental nature apart from the sacraments designated by each church. This means that they are recognized as a privileged space for uniting with God, though this does not mean that other moments in life cannot have a similar value. In our evangelical tradition, the practice of personal and communal prayer can be considered as having this sacramental nature. The same can be said of the community worship service or the study of the word of God.

It is more difficult for us (though not for the Catholic and Orthodox traditions) to speak of the church as a sacrament. In this entity that exists between two dimensions where the human encounters the divine, the evangelical understanding tends to emphasize the human element of the church—and therefore the aspect of its *becoming* the church the Lord wants it to be—whereas other traditions prefer to emphasize the aspect of the church as a creation of God—the body of Christ—and thus they enhance what the church *already is*. There's a well-known expression about the kingdom of God being among us "already, but not yet"; when applying it to the church, we evangelicals emphasize the "not yet" while Catholic and Orthodox theologies focus on "already."

Yet, there is an evangelical "already" we wish to examine in this chapter and that might well be considered an action with a sacramental nature. We are referring to the proclamation of the word. One of the discoveries of the Reformation of the sixteenth century, from which the evangelical movement derives (in a general sense), is the central place of the word in the life and testimony of the believer and the church. What we call "word" has two meanings in our discourse: one refers to the Scriptures and the other to Christ (the *logos* in the Greek language of the New Testament). Thus, to proclaim the word is both to make known the Holy Scriptures and to announce Christ as savior and Lord of the world; however, we should avoid the ambiguous and improper use of the term and clearly establish that the church is constituted under the rule of Christ (the Word, the *logos*) that we come to know through the Scriptures (the "Word" of God, sometimes spelled with a lowercase letter so as to differentiate them, though here we prefer the use of a capital letter). So, we preach Jesus, the Christ, just as he is introduced and witnessed to in the biblical texts. It is important to bear this in mind since, because of our theological education and evangelical doctrinal heritage, the temptation always exists to confuse the Bible with Christ and so fall into a kind of "bibliolatry." If we confuse the word (the Scripture) with the Word (Christ), we lose sight of the main reason for the existence of the church.

And the Lord Said

The phrase "and the Lord said" resounds time and time again in the prophetic books of the Old Testament. When a prophet wanted to confront the people with the direct message of God, and at the same time provoke an answer, he would start or end his speech with that phrase. The same meaning was applied to "oracle of the Lord" or "oracle of Yahweh (or Jehovah)." What do these expressions mean?

In the prophetic texts we find a wide variety of literary genres and forms, and all of them aim to transmit a particular message of God to the people. When the expression "the Lord said" or "oracle of the Lord" is used, the purpose is to point out to the listener that what is being said is the very Word of God for his life and situation. It is a way to warn him that he should pay special attention because the message is fundamental for his present and future. There are in the prophetic texts different objectives: while some introduce a word of condemnation and punishment, others announce the imminent salvation and blessing that will be shed over the people. It is necessary to remember that those texts that we identify as condemnatory have, in the end, the intention to save those who are far from the will of God, inviting them to consider it carefully. So it is that, ultimately, all the texts are about salvation if we understand that when our mistakes and sins are shown to us we are rescued from sinking deeper into them.

In the New Testament there is no equivalent expression, probably because Jesus himself is the Word. Each verse in the gospels announces "God's Word for your life and situation" and therefore it is not necessary to explicitly mark it. Though there are some expressions—such as "you have heard that . . . *but I say to you*" (Matt 5), or "he began to teach them many things *in parables*" (Mark 4:2), or "after Jesus had finished *all his sayings*" (Luke 7:1)—that seem to distinguish between occasional conversations and those moments when the Lord was delivering a specific teaching and special attention was needed. So that even in the work of Jesus we find that certain moments and certain words were meant to be received with special attention, and thus the narrative of the gospels have empasized and marked them explicitly. We could say that not only the prophetic literature but also the gospels can distinguish the general discourse from the moment when the Word is announced with particular emphasis. This being the case, it should not be strange that today we are called to reproduce that attitude, and that in the church's practice this becomes real through the concrete action of what is called the proclamation of the Word. In the act of preaching and announcing the Word, the church is stating that this is the core of its message and that, instead of gold and silver, it is delivering the most valuable thing it has, which has been given as a treasure that behaves quite strangely: it dwindles if you are stingy with it, and the more you share it, the more it increases.

Preaching the Word

The sacramental dimension of the proclamation of the Word should be expressed in the whole life of the church and finds its place of ultimate clarity in the action of preaching. When the preacher addresses the congregation, he or she should be conscious that he or she is being used by the Holy Spirit to proclaim the good news of God and to invite those who come near to embrace the faith and to listen to his or her preaching. Once again, the Lord uses men and women and through their voices He presents a message that transcends our capacities and expresses the will of God—not our own will—to those who are listening. It is again the same mystery ("sacrament") of knowing that we are being used by something superior to us and that we cannot own; we can only act as speakers for the divine. The preacher must do whatever he or she can in order to make the pulpit a privileged place to communicate what the Lord has to say to His people and at the same time challenge everybody—even those who do not place faith at the center of their lives—to be confronted with the message of salvation. Given that we recognize that preaching is a sacramental space, it is striking that we have reflected so little on its practice and content. There are certain elements that help this space acquire its dimension. Let's analyze some of them, bearing in mind that this list is not comprehensive and seeks to introduce us to a consideration that should be enlarged and deepened beyond these pages.

Two elements should be avoided when preaching. The first is the temptation for the church to preach about itself. This has two different aspects: when preaching emphasizes the goodness of the church and places it as an example before the world, and—this other aspect is more subtle—when preaching becomes ecclesiocentric, that is, locates the church in the place that should be occupied by Christ, the Word. We believe it is not necessary to comment on the first aspect since it is obvious that it is not compatible with the gospel. It is the second aspect that should give us pause. All preaching should remind us that the community of faith is instrumental to the kingdom and the Word, and by no means an end in itself. Thus we acknowledge that the church lives in the hope of being transformed and so becoming the definitive church the Lord wants it to be. But while this is not so, the permanent presence and support of the Spirit is the referent that gives life and meaning to it. Consequently, the proclamation should always be directed at introducing Christ who gave us His Spirit to accompany us through this time and that will not leave His church alone or stop correcting its mistakes and failures. Remembering that the church is a space created by God to announce His Word should prevent us from mistaking this space with the content, thus avoiding the risk of depriving it of all value. We may think that this risk is closer to the Catholic understanding than the Protestant one—and no doubt there are reasons to think this way—but in the evangelical practice there also exists the temptation to think that the community of which we are a part is the complete and definitive church, without feeling the need to understand ourselves as a part of a larger body that Christ encourages and that constitutes His people disseminated around the world.

The second element to avoid is this: the preacher should not think that the content of his preaching must be whatever he or she believes about a certain biblical text. The pulpit is not a platform for the exposition of our own ideas, likes, and leanings about the text in front of us. Preaching should not be transformed into a discourse in which the latest theological novelties are tested. It is obvious and reasonable that all preaching is built on the beliefs and experiences of the preacher, but this must not make us forget that the heart of all proclamation is to present the good news of God to the people. The preacher is not there to show his wisdom or boast of having read the latest papers on theology, no matter how excellent they are. Preaching should take into account that the text should be preached in the context of the community to which it is addressed, and the latter in its double dimension of the community itself and of the world in which the community lives and develops its ministry. Thus, the thinking of the preacher must go through different stages that will shape his message according to the material and spiritual needs of the community receiving his words. Many are the paths on which people walk, and many the needs of God's people in the world, but what is said there should be the product of a long process of reflection in which the Word shines as the destination of every path. The preacher may not know the starting point of every listener, but he should be clear on the arrival point to which his word should lead them.

We should also refer to the sacramental action of the proclamation of the Word in a positive sense. There are three other elements that we would like to mention. The first is that every sermon must place itself under the judgment of God and be ready to be imbued with the Word. It will be a humble word, conscious that there is something higher than itself and that its function is to be good salt so as to go out as it should, and that we should be the best administrators of God's assets so that they are multiplied. Also, "the proclamation of the Word" will have to be aware of the difference between the terms "the proclamation" and "the Word." The first refers to what we have to do and our disposition of putting ourselves in God's hands, so that we are instruments that perform His will. The tools are the gifts we have been given and the recognition of the church that allows us to direct ourselves to it and the world, in the confidence that we will be—within our human limitations—faithful interpreters of the message. The second term, "the Word," will be the referent, the ultimate content and aim of the discourse. The proclamation must be mainly expositive of what the biblical text says and tries to convey. We have nothing to add to the Word so that it becomes efficacious or so that it meets its end of offering salvation and abundant life to all people. Any effort to improve its image or to adapt it—according to our understanding—to a better form and one more related to our time runs the risk of turning it into an object for our liking and, consequently, twisting it. The Word is not always the word that we want, but the one it wants to be.

The second element can be framed by this question: by which authority does the preacher proclaim the Word? This is not a simple question since the human dimension of proclamation is not canceled out; however, we are transmitting something that does not belong to us, because it belongs to God. In our opinion, the authority to preach should come neither from us nor from the church. The church complies with its task in recognizing the preacher as God's spokesperson and a suitable interpreter for its times, and it expresses that—though not exclusively—in the ordination for the ministry of Word and sacrament; but the authority to preach is not a certificate obtained prior to the very act of preaching that anyone can exhibit and possess and that confers the ineffable power to interpret the Scriptures. In our understanding, the preacher's authority consists of the strength of the message proclaimed and is an essential part of the sacramental moment when the Word authorizes itself to be announced and presented to the world. Thus, the preaching is supported by its own content. There is no institution or charismatic individual that can replace this condition of being the living Word that reveals itself and shows its efficacy in the ability to change the life of the person who receives it.

The last element to be mentioned is, perhaps, one of the marks of Protestantism and the evangelical movement: the confrontation of the listener with the crucified and resurrected Christ. The Word is announced in a positive way, as an invitation to be transformed by this reality that breaks in on the person. It is a recognition that grace abounds where the Word is proclaimed and accepted, the intimate conviction that where it has not yet germinated, the seed sleeps while it waits for a better moment. It is this encounter with Jesus that gives meaning to preaching and constitutes the church as it is. When we say from the pulpit "this is the Word of God," we are not utilizing an ornamental phrase but announcing—with fear and trembling, we hope, but firmly—that God is among us and has something to say to us.

12

From What Does Christ Save Us?

The church proclaims Christ as the savior and redeemer of the world. It announces that He came "so that everyone who believes in him may not perish" (John 3:16). It says that "Christ Jesus came into the world to save sinners" (1 Tim 1:15) and adds that "God decided, through the foolishness of our proclamation, to save those who believe" (1 Cor 1:21). The texts could be multiplied and still they would be in agreement on the central affirmation that Christ brings salvation to people and creation. What does this mean?

It is obvious that in talking about the salvation and redemption of someone it can be supposed that his situation is such that he needs that redemption. Only what is lost can be saved, or what is broken redeemed, but while this form of expression is clear enough when we speak of everyday situations (saving the crew from shipwreck, rebuilding a ruined house, salvaging a friendship broken by circumstances, restoring a work of art in danger of deteriorating, etc.) we must ask ourselves what the meaning of the gospels is when applied to people's lives. The question is crucial because it is related to salvation, the central message announced by the church that gives meaning to its existence. If we cannot answer this question, our whole discourse runs the risk of being void.

Usually, in our churches we rejoice when our brothers and sisters testify to the beneficial effects of having accepted faith in Christ. There are all kind of experiences, and in some cases they tell terrible stories of alcoholism, drug addiction, abuse in the family and child abandonment, all of them being overcome by the new life initiated at the moment they get to know Christ and apply the ethics of the gospel. In such cases, the message of salvation is clear and it applies to situations of degradation of life and of the more elemental social relationships.

In the Epistle to the Romans (5:20) we are told that where sin abounded, grace likewise abounded, which shows that the more we move away from God, the greater God's effort to rescue us, and that no sin can exceed God's love in His effort to save the sinner. This is beyond doubt and needs no commentary.

The question that remains to be answered is, "What is the meaning of salvation for the mulititude of people who are not criminals, or are not violent to their relatives, or do not fall into prostitution?" Does a person who leads a normal, healthy life, loves his family, takes care of his body and promotes solidarity among his neighbors need to be saved? Does the church have something to say, in the gospel that it preaches, to the honest woman who fulfills all her obligations, is kind to her neighbors and sensitive to injustices, with no reference to a religious faith? What does Christ save this man or this woman from?

What Is Sin?

We are all sinners, and salvation frees us from sin. The narrative in Genesis 1:1–11 describes how God created the human being in harmony with Himself and nature, and how man's conduct has separated him from that relationship. The immoderation expressed in the story of Adam and Eve, the murder of Abel, the violence against the weak are scenarios that show how human sin moves persons away from God and places them in a position of conflict with their neighbors and nature. In the end, this conduct leads to a conflict against one's own self, as Paul says: "For I do not do the good I want, but the evil I do not want is what I do" (Rom 7:19). This situation of being estranged from God and His plan for each person is what we call sin. This situation multiplies in small and great things, from personal meanness and envy to the orchestration of wars and economic planning that leaves millions of people in misery; from the daily lie to sexual abuse; from the deterioration of faith through carelessness to religious fanaticism.

Defining sin is not an easy task. Let's put it like this: sin is like an abyss in the soul where we should have cadence, or like a silence that dominates space when we are waiting to encounter a voice. If there is sin, then something has failed—and if we look into it carefully we will find that what has failed is the relationship that should link the person to God's expectation for him. When we sin we are like an Stradivarius that has gone out of tune: made of the best wood, but shabby and incomplete, it cannot reach the aim it was created for and finally does not play the music its creator is longing to hear. Sin is a rupture and it manifests in the deterioration of the relationship between what God has prepared for our lives and the path we have decided to take.

Sin is always stronger than we are. This statement might not be clear for many people, but it is clear for God, who, when setting us free from such shortcomings, sent His Son to give His life and in doing so completed ours. Thus understood, the action of God in Christ consists of saving our lives from sin and providing us with a presence that offers a new direction and meaning to our days, restoring the relation between our life and God's reality, so that we can live the promise as such and not as an unfounded, illusory expectation.

The question still remains whether salvation attained through Christ eliminates our sin or whether—to a certain extent—it remains. Our opinion is that the defeat of evil shown in the cross is total and definitive; what is not complete is our acceptance of the good news and its consequences for our lives. That is the reason why we say that we live by the grace of God, but sin remains in us. They are sinners—and not those who consider themselves saintly and pure—who recognize they need God in their lives and cry out for help because they know they cannot defeat the evil that tears them apart from God and from a healthy relationship with their neighbors. The good news of salvation is that we are all rescued and freed from evil and invited to rebuild our relationship with God. When we say the Lord cleanses us from sin we are saying that it is because of His merits and His strength that sin can be defeated in us. Consequently, the believer starts living according to the reality of being free from emptiness and death, though those forces still remain in him.

Salvation, Here and Hereafter

For centuries, Christian theology has considered life on earth a trial period to demonstrate whether the person was worthy of saving or not. In this conception the empasis is placed on the afterlife, where on the one hand there is a place in which the saved will enjoy the eternal grace bestowed by God (paradise, heaven) and, on the other hand, a place in which those who have not accessed this benefit would be lost forever. This interpretation of life as an exercise in showing kindness in order to obtain a heavenly prize has reinforced the idea that exists in certain forms of ancient culture that everything related to the here and now is marginal and incidental and deserves no consideration, unless it is linked to achieving some place in eternal life.

In this way human progress is devalued, both in social and cultural relationships and in the search for pleasure and good taste, as they are considered distractions from that which really should interest the person in the fundamental project of acquiring salvation and eternal life.

The reaction to this conception was expressed in almost opposite terms. It can be explained as follows: there is nothing we can say about eternal life or what happens after we are dead, and we should not care about it. We can only testify as believers about what has to do with this life in the here and now, for which the Lord gave Himself on the cross. When it comes to what will happen after death, we can only trust that God will not abandon us.

This way of understanding Christian faith emphasizes personal and social ethics and its consequences in life for individuals and peoples. It insists that God is interested in what happens to us in this life and that He has answers for today's problems. It is usually pointed out that good acts of solidarity and justice should be performed, not to win a place in heaven, but out of compassion for and commitment to those who suffer and need our help, and that the core of Christian faith consists in being an instrument for living this life in harmony with God and our neighbors and so helping to humanize the world by working for peace and justice.

In our opinion, these two points of view are not mistaken because of what they say but because of what they do not say. Each of them emphasizes one real and correct aspect of salvation, but they go only halfway; they obscure each other and thus limit the extension of the action of salvation that bursts into history in all of its dimensions. In other words, the first one explains the transcendent aspect of the gospel and the second its immanent aspect. It is also necessary to note that this misconception diminishes our understanding of each proposal and, consequently, neither the transcendent nor the immanent aspect of the gospel is properly represented by either of them. How can we solve this dilemma?

There are several ways to approach this issue, and we have chosen to deal with it through the issue of the Trinity. We are doing so because it is a fundamental doctrine of Christianity and because it is accepted by almost all the Christian churches (with a few exceptions). We perceive that in both conceptions there is a reduction of one of the persons in the Trinity in relation to the attributes of one of the others. When we consider Christian life just an exercise toward eternal life, the human dimension of God expressed through His Son Jesus of Nazareth dissolves, and the person of the Son becomes instrumental to the role of the Father. If God is eternal and unchanging, if it is He who judges us and gives us a destiny after our physical death, then the *only* function of Jesus is to be a living example so that we, when imitating Him, acquire the right to eternal life. His "true man" condition is diminished to the accessory function of showing us how we should behave in order to please the Father and recieve His benefits.

The problem is that in this perspective—which is presented as more "spiritual"—the person of Jesus Christ loses His transcendent dimension and is reduced to what we can learn from him and to our ability to imitate Him. It also diminishes the fact that what Christ did—the way to salvation opened by Him—cannot be repeated and does not require or depend on our suffering. Thus, the concept of "imitation of Christ"—so cherished by this conception—must be qualified in order to avoid turning it into a misunderstanding of the idea that the believer lives by the grace of the sacrifice already committed and consummated and by the resurrection that followed the cross. We are called to announce the good news of the gospel given to us by Christ, but not to imitate the sacrifice of the Son. It goes without saying that we are not denying the worth of believers who, yesterday and today, have given their lives for the cause of the gospel, but it is necessary to understand that, in those cases, suffering was not sought but was produced by circumstances in which martyrdom was the only way to remain faithful to the Lord. Suffering and death on account of faith are the result of hostility and human violence, and are not a condition given by God for the salvation of people.

On the other extreme, when we limit our concern to what is going on in this life, we lose the cosmic dimension of the person of the Father, and this does not allow us to perceive that His role starts with creation and is completed in the final encounter with all of creation in Himself. In theological terms, what has happened is that the eschatological dimension of God has diminished and, in certain aspects, He takes on the attributes of the Son. In this model God is considered Creator, giver of life, and sustainer of history, but His role seems to be limited to giving us His Son for the sole purpose that we organize our life on earth in accordance with His will. It reduces the incarnation of Jesus to only one aspect—the human one—and leaves the "true God" dimension of the Son weakened.

So, this emphasis on immanence prefers to understand the resurrection of Christ in terms of a symbolic prolongation of life in other historical and social actors: people, descendants, the church, art, the return to dust in order to be reborn in nature, etc. But, despite all of these aspects being rich in significance and valuable for the humanity they represent, they do not express the gospel message that the Son has a place ready for those who trust Him and surrender their bodies to the earth.

Eternal Life for Whom?

Out of the discussion above arise two things we wish to comment on here. The first is that, even if we understand that there is continuity between our earthly life—what we are today—and eternal life, there is no sense in trying to describe what that eternal life will be like. That reality surpasses our understanding and reason and yet we must not deny its existence. It has been said that the cells of the retina "understand" colors, but if I wished to explain to them what a melody is they would have no way of understanding me. And which words would we use to explain colors and shapes to the cells in our ear? With eternal life we experience the same thing. Our faculties are not prepared to clearly understand this dimension, and the Lord Himself invites us to believe and trust that God's plan will be good for us and will meet all our needs and expectations.

The second is whether we understand salvation as universal (i.e., for everyone) or only for those who have fulfilled the will of God. Those who believe the former assume that God, in His love, will take into account the social and psychological conditions that give rise to evil and, further, that not all harmful actions were conceived in this way but many times were the result of well-intended actions or seeing the dynamics of life from a narrow perspective. It is understood that people act with kindness or out of hatred because they are motivated by very deep feelings that only God can work out, and that—finally—forgiveness and compassion will prevail over punishment.

Those who think that salvation is only for some have on their side a large selection of biblical texts and are convinced that in fact we are fully responsible for our personal actions, whether they were moral or related to the gospel: those who accepted the faith and lived according to it will be rewarded, and those who did not will not enjoy such a reward.

It is obvious that the issue is a difficult one, not only because it has to do with matters that are to a certain extent abstract but fundamentally because it involves all of us, since it is impossible to talk about it without—perhaps unconsciously—dealing with our own final destiny. On the other hand, it is necessary to avoid the common mistake of making our own list of the saved and the condemned, giving the church—or, in some cases, individuals—the role that only God can play. From the shameful auto-da-fés of the past to the marginalization of communion in the church today, the practice of judging with human criteria what can only correspond to divine wisdom has deteriorated the witness of the church and the credibility of its message. But the biblical message again and again maintains that there are different destinies for the righteous and for sinners. What can we say to this? In our opinion, we find a way toward a solution if we assume that we can talk about salvation and condemnation only in a positive sense. That is, the task of the church is to announce the good news of salvation in the positive sense: God is love and seeks to shed His grace upon us and redeem us by cleansing us of sin and freeing us from death. Also, we can positively affirm that those who have accepted the gospel rest in the Lord and have been received by Him. We can clearly say that every believer has been redeemed by God and enjoys here, in this life, the firstfruits of His love and will fully enjoy His company when the Lord calls him to His presence. But we cannot speak with authority in the negative sense, pointing to who will not receive God's love or will not have a place in His home. We have not been given the capacity to know which criteria God will apply to judge those individuals who, to our understanding, have lived apart from Him. We may affirm God's condemnation of sin, but we must be careful not to extend that condemnation to the sinner, who, on the contrary, the gospel invites us to understand and love; otherwise, we run the risk of doing something the Lord has not called us to do and for which He has not prepared us.

13

For What Does Christ Save Us?

One of the characteristics of the Christian faith is that the salvation announced and worked out by Christ has a particular purpose. Salvation gives new meaning to the life of the believer and manifests itself by redirecting his life so that God's love and His message become what moves and gives meaning to our days. As such, salvation is not a specific way of life, nor can it be understood as a unique, superior state of the soul that embellishes our religious experience. Neither is it a particular, intermediate state on the way to something more sublime and distant. Any of these situations implies a reduction of Christian salvation to a practice, a spirituality, or a particular liturgy inevitably framed in cultural forms that will pass away. Salvation—which implies all these areas of life and even more—must not be confused with any of the *forms* in which human experience expresses this reality. On the contrary, the salvation performed by the grace of God acts in us, saving our life and changing it in such a way that now we must refer to the reality of the kingdom and the good news of salvation.

Rescuing the Days and the Hours

One of the first implications of experiencing salvation is to realize that in God nothing is lost. He rescues our steps. Those things we love are not destined to be consumed by the fire that reduces all to ashes because there, where we have placed our heart and life, remains an indelible trace that cannot be perceived by us and that does not depend on our insufficient memory. The Lord rescues everything good and keeps it because that is the trace of what we have been and of what He wants us to be. Thus, the believer lives with the intimate belief that, in some inexplicable way, the worn stone will recover its brilliance, the voice that gave us the greatest poetry will ring out again, and that afternoon or night that touched us so deeply, forever, will not perish with the last remains of our fragile existence.

The cross and the resurrection announce that the exceptional moment when Christ gave his life for us was one of sublime love that redeemed all those moments when human love has been and is present. Because the incarnation—and the exaltation of the human that it implies—is not only the incarnation of the body but also of human time, the days and hours in which we work out our existence, so his agony and resurrection act as a definite and full counterbalance in order to rescue from death all those valuable things that deserve not to be forgotten. And it does so not only for the important things, but particularly for those that go unnoticed by almost everyone. He rescues this caress, that complete devotion, the word given at the right time, the gesture that raises the fallen from darkness. In the certainty of salvation there is no room for lamenting the loss of what was, if we have expressed love and solidarity and if we have offered the best of ourselves.

Thus, that which we left behind in the past and which we soon will not be able to recall is rescued by God and preserved as testimony of the works of love that are not lost but prosper and remain, even without our being aware of it, as narrated in Matt 25:31–46, where those who loved God through acts of kindness were not aware of it ("When was it that we saw you hungry and gave you food?" they asked Jesus)—and are surprised to know that He recovered those acts that they themselves had forgotten. God distinguishes between that which merits eternity and that which will be forgotten and perish like "the grass of the field," which in the biblical fields lasts for no more than a brief season.

The Project of God

In the certainty that works of love are rescued by God and that they defeat death, the Christian feels that he or she can devote his or her life to God's project. Similarly, we have the certainty that we have been rescued from the power of sin and this calls us into new ways of relating to our neighbors and to God Himself; but that which God expects from His children is not only a personal act but one that involves the whole church. To have a clear idea of God's project for life is also to contribute to the testimony of the church, thus leading our relationship with Christ, which is personal and nontransferable, to be transformed into our contribution to the greater development of the mission of Christ's church in the world.

To refer to God's project for our lives is to refer to what He expects from the believer, and it is risky to try to reduce it to a few lines, particularly because we might disagree on the features of such a project. Yet, we can say that there are certain elements on which Christianity agrees.

Living in accordance with the gospels entails placing our faith in Christ, loving God and neighbor, seeking justice for everyone, being in solidarity with the poor and marginalized, waiting with confidence for the day when the Lord will call us to a new life. If we review this summary—which is no doubt a simplification—we will note that there are two dimensions: one of faith and one of ethical consequences. We believe in Jesus Christ, we believe in eternal life, and we love God, whom we cannot see. But we work for justice, we are in solidarity with those in need, and we love our neighbor, whom we can indeed see. In this way God's project for the life of the believer has these two dimensions.

We will devote some thinking to each of the dimensions. Salvation, received and recognized, empowers us on the one hand to increase and mature in our faith, to deepen it throughout our lives, walking on a path where there is always a higher step to climb. Then it is not only about believing but knowing in which God we believe and who this Christ is we are testifying to. It goes without saying that the gospel warns against assuming that because we say "Lord, Lord" (Matt 7:21) we are already participating in God's project, since next comes a clause of verification: "only the one who does the will of my Father." Thus, the faith we proclaim with our mouths should be confirmed in the concrete practice of doing the will of God.

On the other hand, the second dimension is related to doing the will of the Father (the ethical aspect of the gospel) and should also be founded in the faith we declare. We love our neighbor because Christ first loved us; we work for justice because God made creation to live in harmony and gave dignity to human beings; we forgive the debts of others because Christ has forgiven our debts. Ethical choices can, in some cases, be shared by other religions and philosophies, but what is unique to the Christian is that, having been rescued by Christ from death and having the certainty of eternal life, he may go beyond his own will and devote his life to the service of his neighbors. The way is open: faith leads to works.

Faith versus Works, or Faith and Works?

The discussion in the paragraph above introduces us to the issue of faith versus works. This was a central question in the discussion during the Reformation led by Martin Luther, and up to the present it has divided the theological waters between those who emphasize one aspect and those who emphasize the other. It is also true that the problem has not always been understood in its true dimension and, therefore, on occasion we have a tendency to lean to one side or the other without taking into account what is at stake. In a nutshell, the matter can be formulated this way: all churches are in agreement that the gospel demands faith and demands conduct in line with such faith ("works"). The point is to discern what the relation is between them, and what the role of faith and of works is in salvation and in God's project.

Until the Reformation, the position accepted by the church was that works contributed to the acquisition of salvation. That is, the believer needed faith to be saved, but faith was not enough and it was necessary to gather merits to gain access to heaven. It was necessary to perform a certain number of works in order to obtain merits that would allow one to get closer to heaven and salvation. These works could be supporting one's neighbors (tending the sick, helping the poor), personal suffering (resigning one's self to pray in the desert, flagellating oneself or giving up the pleasures of the flesh), or contributing goods to the church (offerings for the building of a sanctuary, giving land).

The practice of acquiring indulgences—which exists to this day in Catholicism—consisted of adding up good works in order to obtain salvation and a place in the kingdom of God after death. There were other ways to acquire salvation through human action, but aside from the misuse of some of these ways, the model has an essential defect: it places the decision of salvation on our side. In this line of thinking, we gain salvation by means of our suffering, or our money, or our love of neighbor.

Thus, God bestows on us the salvation *we deserve* for the merits we have accumulated by multiplying works and effort and, consequently, salvation becomes a right, like the right of any person who buys a property and then demands that his ownership of it be recognized. In the best of cases it is understood as a reward (God rewards my sufferings with eternity in the afterlife). In the worst of cases—which was not an exception but a rule—as a heavenly transaction: I give this to God and He pays me with salvation. Also, we have to consider the opposite, as if God were saying: because you did not give me such a thing, I will not reward you with salvation. Everything is exacerbated by the human administration of these heavenly transactions in which the Christian church shows its worst side.

Confronted with such a theology—which, though revised and lacking the most aggressive edges, is still, in general terms, current in the Catholic Church—the Reformation offered an alternative for understanding the relationship between faith and works. Its assertion is that salvation is by grace, a gift made out of love, and nothing we might do can modify or bring nearer this gift from God. Through his death on the cross and his resurrection, Christ did everything that is necessary for our salvation and He demands nothing. What kind of gift is it if we are asked to pay? The believer is invited to believe in the gospel, in Christ's death and resurrection for our sins, and it is this faith that gives the certainty and peace of mind of the salvation God has offered on our behalf. Once the believer knows and experiences the gratuity of salvation and he discovers that nothing is asked in return, he begins to understand that this faith is what moves him to love his neighbor and to act accordingly. He has experienced a love-act from God, and that love can neither be hidden nor accumulated in our spiritual pockets. Therefore works are the consequence of having received the love and certainty of salvation, and not the price to be paid to acquire it.

From this point of view there is no room to presume that through our good works and effort we have gained the right to salvation, and even less to demand it, because the act of salvation performed on the cross is of such magnitude that it will not be possible to pay, not even with our whole life, because—and this is what really matters—God does not expect any retribution from us for the shedding of his grace. In short, we can say that the works of faith are the response of the believer in gratitude to God for the salvation already received and that they emerge when he knows and experiences God's love.

Which Faith, Which Works?

Here it is necessary to do two things. The first is to analyze which works we are referring to. From the evangelical point of view the only "works" worthy of being a response to God's saving action are those related to and motivated by the love of neighbor and the love of God. Voluntary suffering is meaningful when it is part of God's project and thus functions to show God's love to our neighbors, but not when it is merely self-flagellation. Giving time or assets is meaningful when it benefits our neighbors or the witness of the church, but not when it is understood as an installment toward my heavenly salvation. We do not pray to acquire heaven but because we have the certainty that we have already been liberated by God from the fear of death, and we raise our prayers of gratitude, praise, or intercession confident that God is attentive to our feelings and needs, with no need to give something in return.

Thus, the works the believer is drawn to do by the gospel as an act of gratitude for salvation are intended to reflect in others the love received from God. There are no secondary intentions. They are not directed to the acquisition of anything, and they will not enhance our position before God or warrant any privileges. They must be free—as is the love of God—in order to be an honest love-act for our neighbors and not a gesture that conceals the search for a reward that has nothing to do with the men and women before us. This is so because actually the believer gives something that does not belong to him since he knows that the love he is sharing he first received from God. If we recognize that life is a gift from God and that we owe Him everything we have and everything we are, there is no reason not to be generous and openhanded in our devotion to and solidarity with those in need around us, and with the church and the whole world. On the other hand, it is also necessary to state that those works that are unrelated to our neighbors or the witness of the church, no matter how well-intentioned, not only do nothing to effect salvation but also waste time, distracting the believer from adopting God's project for his life.

Second, we must remember that in the evangelical tradition we run the risk of believing that if salvation is by faith—and works themselves do not contribute to salvation—it is possible to lead a life of faith without works, which—according to our understanding—would mean without the ethical consequences of Christian faith. The definition of salvation as grace freely received should cancel that possibility since, in the face of the immensity of the gift, a gesture of gratitude is an inevitable consequence. Yet, in some sectors of the evangelical population, which are prone to adopt a very narrow theology that sometimes does not contemplate the double dimension of God's project for each believer's life, it is possible to arrive at such a situation. Obviously, this is a theoretical attitude, not a practical one, since it is not possible to live a biblical life without texts like "love your neighbor as yourself" (Luke 10:27) or "blessed are those who hunger and thirst for righteousness" (Matt 5:6), which move the believer to act accordingly or simply fall into a distortion of the faith they intend to profess. But no matter how theoretical or absurd it might appear, we should not minimize its risk and potential presence in our churches. In our opinion, to avoid this mistake it is necessary to point out that works are a visible consequence of the faith that is invisible. So whoever invokes the strength of his faith, but does not verify that faith through visible works, probably is not sufficiently mature in his belief, or he has a picture of his faith that is superior to his actual faith. Works are the fruit of faith and are, at the same time, its verification. When we believe, we love God and our neighbor, and when we do so works inevitably emerge that express this way of understanding faith and life. If they are not present it is because something is wrong in that faith or in that life.

14

Our Faith and Our Mission: The Pond Begins to Tremble

The water in the pond is still and there is no demand for change. Everything seems to be all right and the few movements that can be perceive are not enough to disturb or threaten its stillness. It has always been like this; no changes are expected. All of a sudden, a pebble falls into the middle of the pond. It is a little stone, almost insignificant. No noise was heard, seemingly nothing has changed, but now a small circle has formed where the pebble fell, and the circle starts expanding; its slight movement generates a new circle. The first circle widens and new circles appear. They ripple the water in the pond and disrupt the calm, awakening the pond. The water is moving. The first circle reaches the edge and crashes. Surprised, the birds fly away and announce that something has happened in the pond. Stillness turns into movement. From the air above the birds have a different view, with an increasing movement always originating from this mysterious, central point. The birds fly far away, they disappear into the infinite sky in all directions and announce that changes are taking place in the pond.

The First Circles: The Person

The challenge expressed in Mark 16:15, "Go into all the world and proclaim the good news to the whole creation," is situated in the center of the pond. In general, it is simple to understand the first circles, the nearest ones. They refer to our personal life, even our private life. The gospel always starts with a personal decision—accepting that the message of Jesus Christ is essential to our life and committing ourselves to live according to His teachings. No one can deny a person the right to decide for himself whether to accept the gospel. The gospel cannot be imposed. Without the first circle the others lose all meaning. It is as simple as this (and let's bear in mind that the traditional preaching of the church has reached this point): today this first circle of personal faith is challenged from two opposite ends. On the one hand is an individualistic current like none ever seen in history, an affirmation that the only things of value are my own exclusive interests, my feelings and my likes. Such individualism implies an indifference toward our neighbors and their problems and fate, and an exaltation of a way of life that ignores any link to other people. With a facade more or less intellectual, this position has theological and philosophical representatives and scarcely conceals that it offers nothing but sheer selfishness. It affirms that only this circle exists and that the others are not related to our faith and salvation.

On the other hand, today we are witnessing an enormous force in the service of destroying the person, making him vanish among the crowd, canceling all difference and creating a sort of new race, culture, and language that pretends at universality but that reveals itself to be a false global village that, in the end, imposes one culture on the others through worldwide media. This path is opposed to the first: the person is destroyed through the denial of the first circle's significance to his private life. As time goes by there is less privacy, the inner circle does not exist, and, consequently, others decide for us.

Broadening the Mission

The latter leads us to the bigger circles, when the gospel expands and includes other portions of reality. We are getting into the sphere of society and culture. The Christian faith is in its best shape to understand the dynamic relationship between faith and culture. All it needs is to review its own history and its origins, in which from the outset the dialogue among cultures and peoples was present. The faith of Abraham, an ancient Semite, was expanded by the hand of Paul, a Jew, in Europe, in those days dominated by the Greco-Roman culture. Later on, it was taken to further lands: Asia, Africa, over the seas, then to America. But from that time in its expansion it did not always comply with its own principles. The church subdued when it should have engaged in dialogue; made war when it should have worked for peace; used force when it should have invited; ignored the dignity of women and placed them in the background, reinforcing the mechanisms of oppression; and fostered hate when it should have loved. Its mouth full of words, it refused to hear the other's voice. No matter how difficult it is to separate the gospel from the cultural container in which it is inevitably presented, today we are conscious that the mission of the church cannot be performed if it is dissociated from the cultures, the languages, and the lives of those we address through the gospel of Christ. In no way is it true that to announce Christ's gospel is to proclaim the superiority of one culture over another; rather, it is to invite one to embody the love of Christ, who will stir the waters of our pond and change our lives according to His Spirit.

It is evident that the circles involving human culture are huge and the gospel cannot be isolated from the political, economic, and social processes of the day. A war is not only the consequence of the rivalry between two peoples or races, but is as common as advertising may induce us to believe. Just look closely and it is easy to find economic interests, histories of oppression, humiliations sometimes lasting centuries imposed by countries or their business representatives that take with them thousands of innocent victims. The external debts that strangle the poor were created under pressure from and for the benefit of the rich, and today are one of the sources of the increasing misery and submission of those who were already struggling simply to survive. The creation of millions of persons excluded from the system of production, condemned to the margins and to the most extreme poverty, leads many individuals to an involuntary delinquency. Our suspicion is that this is not the undesirable consequence of the economic system but a conscious and deliberate political decision to accelerate the concentration of wealth and power in a few hands, undoing decades of labor and union achievements and creating modern and increasingly subtle forms of slavery.

More Rings: The Community and the World

God, the creator of the pond, cares for everything. Let's remember that He says, "Go into all the world," and whoever accepts His message cannot avoid such responsibility. Then we discover that there are other circles beyond these: the environment, being a woman or a man, the impact of new mediums of communication. We Christians cannot disregard the voices of scientists all over the world who warn of the rapid deterioration of life on earth and its consequences. Life on this planet is in danger; however, no one hears the cries of those who are trying to put an end to this infernal process. The destruction of forests, the plundering of the seas, and the indiscriminate exploitation of species on the verge of extinction continues.

Humankind is slowly becoming aware—and at a very high cost—that in different cultures and through diverse ways and mechanisms, women have received neither the same treatment nor the same rights as men. Today we can say that there has been humiliation and discrimination and that the process of establishing equality between men and women is not only a demand of social ethics, but for Christians should be a response to the biblical truth that God created us "male and female" (Gen 1:27) and blessed us in equal measure. We may continue analyzing the bigger circles: the impact of the media that brings us closer and separates us at the same time; the information gap that allows us to watch a war live and prevents us from knowing what is going on in nearby towns; the situation of children who are more and more vulnerable and of young people who have no hope or vision for the future. What kind of society awaits us and what is the Christian answer to this reality? How long will we wait before we begin denouncing the foolishness of a world divided into countries that increase in strength and others that grow weaker, endangering all of life on earth?

More on the Christian Mission

When, at the end of each gospel, Jesus instructs His disciples to continue the mission, He gives them two things: a *task* ("Go into all the world") and a *promise* ("I will be with you"). The task is an activity to be carried out, an action, or better, a series of actions we are entrusted with. The promise is an invitation to faith, to believe in faith, since this is not a visible or material action. How does our faith in the promise of Jesus relate to the task He has entrusted us with, that is, our mission?

Sociology has shown that every project, in order to be carried out, needs a spiritual basis, something some people call *mysticism*, a "something else in addition to planned actions" that gives a transcendent meaning to what we do. Thus, from the building of a community center to the organization of a political project, these actions are based on specific spiritual values that bring together and direct the will of the people. Usually, we hear that such-and-such a project is the result of the passion of a group of persons who are in love with it and whose strength drives the rest toward achieving that dream. The first thing is the project, and then comes the mystical, the passion for carrying it out.

Yet, when it comes to our faith, we find that the order has been reversed. We Christians are not a people with a mission in search of a spiritual basis to give meaning to our actions. We do not envision a task and then go out to convince our neighbors that there is a transcendent foundation for our actions. We have a spirituality founded on the belief that the Holy Spirit will be with them "until the end of the age," and this faith leads them to develop a project in the surrounding community, to address the church's mission. This spirituality is built from the faith in God's promises and with the confidence that He will not abandon His people. Then, and as a consequence of having received grace and in gratitude to God, the believer understands that the mission of announcing and living the gospel, including its ethical and relational aspects, is not a moral duty but a free action in response to everything we have already received (and we remain confident that *we will receive*). Because once we accept the presence of God in our lives, we see not only what this signifies in our past and present, but in the confidence that the future also is in His hands. This is what Psalm 23 means when it says, "Even though I walk through the valley of the shadow of death I fear no evil." These words do not express gratitude for what has already happened in life, but a deep confidence in what the future holds, the fruit of the experience of having walked in faith up to that moment.

Yet, even having experienced that confidence, the Lord respects our personality and autonomy and allows us to ask ourselves: Are we interested in the task of declaring Christ's dominion over economic, racial, cultural, and political interests? Are we willing to pay the price of going against the current that says that it is not possible to do otherwise, to seek another destiny or build another society, or that we should resign ourselves to this, the lesser of evils? (Although one wonders how it can be the lesser of evils, as it condemns millions to despair, hunger, and death.) The possibility always exists to refuse to be part of the mission, to stay at home and become mute and deaf witnesses of how the world falls apart and society condemns itself to meaninglessness.

At the same time we pose these questions it is good to remember that, if we are true disciples of Christ, there are not many choices on this path. Just as the Lord said to Matthew, "Follow me," and he could do nothing but follow the life-project he was invited to, in the same way our mission is not one path among others or a possibility that is interchangeable with others. Rather, we must call it an *irresistible invitation* to become Christ's followers and incorruptible witnesses of the Word of life and hope He has proclaimed. Thus, this spirituality and this mysticism will not be secondary and additional ingredients of the missionary task, but will be the very essence of the action. They will be a part of the mission and will nurture it, and at the same time will be critical (or self-critical) in order to prevent any deviation from it. They will not function as a separate element but as that which forms an indivisible and unique body together with our whole life and mission.

The Mission: Sharing Tasks

The task entrusted to the church is great and we cannot address it alone. Now we wish to point out three aspects of the Christian mission that should be taken into account in order to realize the necessary participation of each believer.

First, we should remember that the Christian mission is a *common* mission for all Christians. It cannot be reduced to ministers, or to two or three persons leading a congregation, or only to our denomination. Peter in Galilee and Paul in Europe developed a simultaneous and common mission, but they were assisted by an anonymous group of converts who accompanied them in every new task and in every place they preached. They had to find the appropriate language for each situation, the examples and symbols that each culture could understand, but the message was the same. Today more than ever we know that we live on a small planet and that the decisions we make in one place affect all of humankind. The Christian church cannot avoid this reality but, on the contrary, should use it to convey a message that addresses the consequences of the actions of some people on others.

Second, God's love is offered to everybody. God loves the fortunate and the poor. He loves the intellectual and the manual laborer, the teacher and the policeman. God's love is for each of them, but the demands are different. God stays by the victim, the dispossessed; God hears the cry of the sufferer. In accordance with our place in society, the gospel presents the ethical obligations we must face. The mission assumed by all also implies a responsibility on the part of those who have gifts (whether material, intellectual, or spiritual) to share them with kindness and generosity. It is interesting to note how sharing generates bonds among believers that the passing of time cannot destroy. If a task is the result of several hands, it will have a quality and a value that the works of an individual will never attain.

Finally, the love of the believer should be broad and generous. The exercise of Christian love is not only the giving away of what we have. What is likely more important and challenging is to be ready to discover the gift the other has to offer me. We are not accustomed to looking for the gifts of others and receiving them as a gift of God for the church. If our brothers and sisters are in need we must help them, but we must also look them in the eyes, because there we will find tremendous riches that will change our lives. Thus we will be happy to discover that the rich are also poor, and that within the framework of Christian faith the poor have riches to share that cannot be bought with money.

Bibliography

Barth, Karl. *Dogmatics in Outline*. Translated by G. T. Thompson. New York: Harper & Row, 1986.

Boff, Leonardo. *Ecclesiogenesis: The Base Communities Reinvent the Church*. Maryknoll, NY: Orbis, 1997.

Grdzelidze, Tamara, ed. *One, Holy, Catholic and Apostolic: Ecumenical Reflections on the Church*. Faith and Order Paper 197. Geneva: WCC, 2005.

Míguez Bonino, José. *Hacia una eclesiología evangelizadora: Una perspectiva wesleyana*. San Pablo: Editeo/Ciemal, 2003.

Moltmann, Jürgen. *The Church in the Power of the Spirit: A Contribution to Messianic Ecclesiology*. Translated by Margaret Kohl. Minneapolis: Fortress, 1993.

World Council of Churches, Commision on Faith and Order. *Called to Be the One Church (The Porto Alegre Ecclesiology Text)*. Geneva: WCC, 2007.

———. *The Church: Towards a Common Vision*. Geneva: WCC, 2013.

———. *The Nature and Mission of the Church: A Stage on the Way to a Common Statement*. Faith and Order Paper 198. Geneva, WCC, 2005.

———. *The Nature and Purpose of the Church: A Stage on the Way to a Common Statement*. Faith and Order Paper 181. Geneva: WCC, 1998.

www.ingramcontent.com/pod-product-compliance
Lightning Source LLC
Chambersburg PA
CBHW032235080426
42735CB00008B/862